"A must read for every college administrator striving to advance their food service program, The Porter Principles is practical, thought-provoking, and readable. College dining is no longer just about the food but how it relates to every campus' need for attention to the three all-important R's—Recruitment, Retention and Alumni Relations."

—J. Michael Floyd, Associate Vice President for Auxiliary Services, University of Georgia

"David's expertise, integrity, professionalism, and commitment to the customer are incomparable. He has the experience and skill to turn concepts into realities, resulting in enormously successful dining programs. David is to program development and contract negotiation what Michael Jordan is to basketball."

—Kathy Welch, C.P.M, Director of Business Services, Rollins College

"David's vision, unrelenting passion and tenacity produced a game changing set of recommendations for our dining program that, since its' successful implementation for Fall 2012, has completely turned around our dining program and has shattered all previous meal plan sales and participation records. The plan profoundly increased and enriched social engagement among our very diverse student population, faculty and staff. When David made his recommendations to campus administrators who were faced with low dining service satisfaction and a very tight deadline , the palpable sense of pessimism regarding the future of the current dining program to-date was met with comments like "exactly what our campus needs". Not only did David's vision produce a bold new cutting edge program and great value for the students, David successfully negotiated a new contract with our incumbent food service operator. It expanded residential dining to 24/7, without increasing mandatory meal plan pricing, all while securing millions of additional dollars from the operator for our University. The new contract was shaped to provide us the needed funds to renovate our dining facilities without holding us hostage to the operator."

—Mark McLaughlin, Executive Director, Ancillary Services,
Simon Fraser University

"My boss gave David high praise as a consultant when he thanked David for telling him "what they did not want to hear" and credited David for being right. Our residential population on has grown dramatically over the past five years with 2,000 new beds planned for the near future. When David realized our available spaces for dining in its current form were going to be inadequate, he put our campus first and proactively came to us with an alternate solution (this was not within the scope of his contract)., David challenged the project team with his bold new vision for our dining program that would support the growth of our population and reinforce the social richness of the neighborhoods we have been attempting to develop on campus. What David developed and recommended was not on any of our radar screens. We are now in the process of implementing his recommendations, and our students and administration have embraced and fully support this new program that we all agree will not only provide our students with a world class dining program, but will transform and enrich the social landscape of our campus for many years to come."

—Mark Kraner, Executive Director, Campus Retail Operations, George Mason University

"David's visionary thinking on dining services contributed to UNH developing a program where 80% of the students could purchase meal plans. His guidance was right on, and we are grateful for his contribution to our successes."

—David J. May, Associate Vice President of Business Affairs,
University of New Hampshire

"David was a consultant that saw and understood our uniqueness. He listened to what our students, parents, alum, donors and staff wanted in a premier dining program. Our administration was so impressed with his ideas that he was rehired (retained) for our new dining center and renovation projects."

—Jane Grant-Shambaugh, Director of Auxiliary Services,
retired, Concordia College

"When David first stepped foot on campus and did a walkthrough, I watched him process everything in sight. I think he has a computer processor in his mind. I have never experienced anything like it in my career. David came to us with forty years of experience in his field. After working with him and listening to his recommendations, it was clear to me that he is the best in his business."

—Robert Rizzuto, Director of Dining Services,
New York Institute of Technology

"When I first met David a few years ago at a convention, I thought his presentation was unbelievable. After spending time with him and his staff, and implementing their recommendations, I can truly say, our dining program has changed dramatically and has become enormously successful. David is truly a visionary!"

—David Keala, Director of Food Services,
BYU-Hawaii

"David, for years we worked together and you told me often that I was your mentor. Now the tables have turned, you are now mentoring me. I am so proud of you and how well you have done."

—Tom Larsen, Founder and Owner,
Pillar House Restaurant

"David provided our university with a new way of looking at our dining program—as a key piece in the student retention puzzle and something that we, as university leaders, not our food service provider, should take the lead in designing. His recommendations for improving our program will add great value along with improved student demand."

—Gerard L. Silberman, Vice President, Administration & Finance,
Kutztown University

"In the mid-nineties our campus was declining in academic quality, student satisfaction, enrollment shortfalls, aging facilities, and sagging morale. While we recognized that our self-operated dining program needed improvement and our dining halls hadn't been updated since the 1960s, as a business officer I knew next to nothing about dining programs. David was a strategic partner in launching an institutional transformation. He assessed our needs, drafted an RFP, and negotiated a tight contract with guaranteed commissions that enabled us to rehab all of our dining facilities and vastly improve the quality, availability and customer loyalty of dining program. Our program and facilities are now a recruitment asset and a showcase for our vendor, thanks to the change process that David made possible."

—Leif Hartmark, Vice President for Finance and Administration, retired, SUNY Oneonta

"Beyond his expertise in food service design, David really understands the core business of our clients. He doesn't settle for the status quo, but rather always encourages us to think outside the box."

—David Hatton, AIA, Vice President, Stantec

"David and his team were instrumental in helping us totally reinvent our food service—our meal plans, our venues, and the selection of a new vendor. Our satisfaction rates soared after implementing Porter's recommendations. We could not be happier with the outcomes!"

—Brenda L. McGee, Vice President, Business & Finance,
St. Bonaventure University

"David is at the top of his class. He definitely enhanced our program for both the students and the University. The dining service experience has improved and the financial return to the University is greater.

—Jesse Batten, CASP, Director of Auxiliary Services,
Coppin State University

"I could see David in this book as if he were still advising us! What you'll read is what you'll get – this is a genuine example of truth in advertising. David promises and he delivers. Our meal plan participation and student satisfaction increased significantly based on changes David proposed. David and his team are a great investment in your ability to recruit, retain, and build relations."

—Gerard A. Tobin, Ph.D., Vice President for Student Life,
Mercyhurst University

"David Porter is a leader in the transformation of dining in higher education. He and his dynamic team challenge their clients to think progressively and creatively ... I was one of those clients. The work he has done in the area of meal plan design and development has helped universities grow their meal plans to rates that exceeded all expectations. We judge our success by how satisfied our students are with the dining program. At the end of the day, that is what truly matters on a college campus.

—Arlene M. Hosea, Assistant to the Vice President for Student Affairs
and Director of Campus Dining Services,
Illinois State University

"In this book David Porter spends a lot of time explaining what he can do to help an institution establish a high quality dining program. I worked closely with David to help move SUNY College at Oneonta from an outdated and tired food service from the late 1990s, to one of the finest dining programs in the state of New York. He does 'talk the talk,' but believe me, he also 'walks the walk.' When contract dining service providers hear that Porter is going to handle the RFP and subsequent negotiations, they start sharpening their pencils and think, 'We're not going to make as much as we thought at this institution.' Because of his detailed analysis of our needs, the structure of the equally detailed RFP, and one of the 'tightest' agreements I have ever seen, we were able to develop a strong partnership with our dining contractor that provides great service to our students, faculty and staff, along with a significant financial return to the campus. The partnership continues to this day."

—Tom Ryder, Executive Director, Ancillary Services,
retired, SUNY Oneonta

"Students and parents love our dining program and beautiful new dining facilities. David and his team were able to listen to the students and SLU campus community to help us develop a very successful dining program which met the majority of the SLU community goals. Without David Porter and his team we could have never made this possible."

—Cindy Atkins, Director of Dining and Conference Service,
St. Lawrence University

"David has the formula to reinvent your dining program. He did it for us, he can do it for you."

—Jeff Pauley, Sr. Director, Dining Services, Spartan Shops Inc.,
San Jose State University

"I have had the privilege of working with Porter/Khouw at three separate college & university settings. Their insight and understanding of how residential dining relates and affects the entire campus community is an understatement. The connection of the residential experience to campus retention cannot be understated. The importance of that first year dining experience also relates to a long term dining customer...even after choosing to move off campus! In two of the campuses where we developed our program with David and his team, both produced positive long term stable financial growth and increased customer satisfaction. In one location our commuter meal plan population went from 400 per year to about 2,000 per year in just under a four year period! David and his team are focused on student engagement and satisfaction by creating well thought out and researched dining solutions."

—Richard Fritz, Director of Residential Dining,
Northern Illinois University

"Ferris State University engaged the services of David and his team of experts to complete a market study and partner with us in the development of a five-year master plan for dining services. Implementation of their recommendations assisted us in 'hitting a grand slam' with our campus community by converting our existing dining program to a model program for colleges and universities, health care operations, K-12 operations, and commercial operations alike. David has exceeded our expectations by becoming very engaged in our campus. His professionalism, expertise, and partnership has been invaluable in the creation of an outstanding dining program at Ferris State University."

—Lori K. Helmer, Director of Dining Services, Auxiliary Enterprises, Ferris State University

"The roadmap to success that David and his team put together for us has been invaluable. It has given us the tools and the direction to further improve our dining program. We are now in the process of a complete renovation of our three dining halls, thanks to David. When we are finished, we will have a state of the art dining program that our students can be proud of."

—Todd Jutila, Director, University Food Services, Montana State University

"David Porter is a visionary in his field. He will tell it to you straight. If you want to improve your institutions' dining experience, while increasing your profitability you would be well served to retain him before your nearest competitor does."

—Mike Steranka, CEO RPS Inc., Author,
Co-Founder, First Income Advisors

"Thanks to the insight and vision of David Porter, our dining program has become an award-winning program with record participation and satisfaction."

—Mike Flory, Director of Food Services,
Hendrix College

"David's grand vision and subsequent recommendations were not on anyone's radar screen and challenging to the conventional wisdom. He also listened to and put our students first. Because of this, he not only proposed a solution that would further increase student participation in dining, but would, for the first time, provide our campus with nothing less than colossal distinction with a meaningful socially rich experience for our students second to none. David's plan did not raise mandatory meal plan pricing to our students; he expanded hours and VALUE and increased our bottom line. David's team has moved ahead with the design of two world class state-of-the-art dining venues on our campus that have been programmed to functionally support our new vision for dining. David is one of a kind in our industry. Thank you David!"

—Jeff Yawn, Director of Eagle Dining Services,
Georgia Southern University

The Porter
Principles

The Porter Principles

Recruit and Retain More Students
and Alumni, Save Millions on Dining,
and Stop Letting the Food Service
Contractors Eat Your Lunch

David Porter

Social Architect™

CEO, President, Porter Khouw Consulting, Inc.
www.PorterKhouwConsulting.com

North America's Leading Independent
Food Service Consulting and Design Firm
for Colleges and Universities

The Library of Congress has catalogued the paperback edition as follows:
Porter, David, 1956 –
The Porter Principles: Recruit and Retain More Students
and Alumni, Save Millions on Dining, and
Stop Letting Food Service Contractors Eat Your Lunch.
Library of Congress Control No: 2013930947

ISBN 978-1-939758-63-7 (paperback)
ISBN 978-1-939758-64-4 (eBook)

Book Cover Design: Ulysses Galgo
Cover Image: Deborah Feingold

Forward all requests to:
David Porter
david.porter@porterkhouwconsulting.com
410-451-3617

CONTENTS

Preface

The first edition of *The Porter Principles* created a thought revolution. In just eleven chapters, I detailed how campus dining, student centers, and housing are the lynchpin to bolstering the all-important "Three R's": Recruitment, Retention, and Alumni Relations. But the truly groundbreaking frontier is what I call the social architecture of a campus—"The Classroom outside of the Classroom"—the way in which schools develop and provide safe and wholesome social space(s) in their facilities that invites face-to-face opportunities for students to develop a meaningful network of new friends and study, collaborate, and problem-solve in engaging ways that may be even more essential to post-graduate success—financial independence—than their course of academic study.

This thought revolution garnered the interest of schools across North America and sparked conversations with administrators, university planners, faculty, and students alike. Over the course of these conversations, I realized that the Porter Principles go beyond improving a university's dining program. In fact, understanding and unlocking the social architecture on campus will enable students and parents to choose the right college, and allow colleges to set their students up for their best chance at success (achieving financial independence) after graduating. And that's what that college degree is all about—creating a better, stronger future for the younger generations that results in a better, stronger, less polarized middle class for America.

That's why I've created this second edition—to include three new thought-provoking chapters that articulate the discoveries I've made through observation and meetings with thousands of people and hundreds of universities across the United States, Canada, and the U.S. Virgin Islands. I hope that you find the ideas contained throughout the book—especially my three new chapters—as groundbreaking and exciting as I do. It is a privilege to be considered a social architecture visionary and thought leader in unlocking the campus planning genetic code so that a university can truly fulfill the goal of producing successful students that are equipped for the ever changing "real world" and are able to achieve financial independence.

About This Book

How can you develop a world class dining program that meets the unique social architecture and dining objectives of your campus? How can you negotiate effectively with food service providers if you let them hold all the cards? Your campus is likely settling for a mediocre dining program that is adversely effecting you recruitment and retention of students and alumni while leaving millions of dollars on the table because the food service providers have all the knowledge and bargaining power.

David's unique approach, vision, and negotiating style has guided North America's top schools to independently create revolutionary dining programs that maximize student participation, increase student and alumni retention.... all while improving a self operated dining program or facilitating a food service provider operator selection process that guarantees high levels of student participation, accountability and protects/produces millions for their campuses.

David's illustrious client list includes University of Georgia, University of New Hampshire, Ferris State University, Wellesley College, Vanderbilt University, Princeton University, University of Notre Dame, Massachusetts Institute of Technology, Brigham Young University, Concordia College, George Mason University, Simon Fraser University, Microsoft Corporation, The United States Naval Academy, and Mt. Sinai Hospital.

David has 40+ years of hands-on foodservice consulting and operations experience.

Acknowledgments

All of my success as an individual, professionally and personally, has come as a result of a massive team effort and fellowship of professional colleagues and the support and love of family and friends. I extend my deepest appreciation and gratitude to:

Michael Steranka, I will be forever grateful for your friendship and personal guidance, and your support in the conception and evolution of this book.

Michael Levin, Sara Stratton and Diane Vo who have spent endless hours over the past 12 months assisting in the production, manuscript editing, and publication of this book.

Cézanne Grawehr was sent to me in the form of divine intervention 16 years ago when she joined my consulting practice. Your professionalism, loyalty, love and friendship have supported me through all of the challenges we have faced as a mere start up to the highly respected North American practice we have achieved today. Cézanne is the glue that holds our company together.

Albin Khouw, my business partner, who in addition to being one of the smartest and nicest people I have ever known, is without exception, the most talented food service designer our industry knows. Your friendship, professionalism and unwavering loyalty over the past 16 years have permitted me, and now our company, to soar to unprecedented heights of success.

Carolyn Watkins, whose knowledge of our industry and of the written word, tireless editing skills and relentless attention to detail and loyalty over the past 11 years has made me, our firm and this book exceptional.

Teresa Potter-Bey, whose knowledge of accounting, and her professional and personal commitment and loyalty to me and our company, has permitted me to focus on our clients as we continue to flourish and grow.

Shaun Rostad has been a senior member of my dream team for the past nine years. I have great respect for Shaun and how he is able to balance his professional life with his wonderful young family. Shaun's relentless attention to detail and willingness to learn and grow has benefited our firm and me greatly. Thank you for your loyalty, tireless efforts professionally and in reviewing and editing this book.

Josh Lazarus is a very committed and well respected member of our planning and marketing team. I appreciate your tireless commitment to support our clients, while dedicating an enormous amount of time and effort in the development, preparation and execution of the marketing and electronic planning and promotion of the book.

Deborah Feingold, who agreed to photograph me for the cover is simply an amazing human being. I was permitted to be in the presence of her greatness and quite literally received the "rock star" treatment. Thank you, Deborah.

To my dream team: Albin Khouw, Cézanne Grawehr, Teresa Potter-Bey, Carolyn Watkins, Shaun Rostad, Josh Lazarus, Roberta Hofmeister, Ron Lisberger, Tanzer Tok and Walter Brinkley. Collectively, the most talented and compelling accumulation of talent in our industry.

To all of my professional colleagues who provided a blurb for this book:

J. Michael Floyd, Associate Vice President of Auxiliary Services, University of Georgia

Michael Flory, Director of Food Services, Hendrix College

Gerald Silberman, Vice President, Administration & Finance, Kutztown University

Jane Grant Shambaugh, Director of Auxiliary Services, retired, Concordia College

Mark Kraner, Executive Director, Campus Retail Operations, George Mason University

Jeff Yawn, Director of Eagle Dining Services, Georgia Southern University

Jesse Batten, CASP, Director of Auxiliary Services, Coppin State University

Mark McLaughlin, Executive Director, Auxiliary Services, Simon Fraser University

Kathy Welch, Director of Business Services, Rollins College

Arlene M. Hosea, Asst. to Vice President for Student Affairs and Director of Campus Dining Services, Illinois State University

Michael Steranka, CEO RPS Inc., Author, Co-Founder First Income Advisors

Brenda L. McGee, Senior Vice President, Business & Finance, St. Bonaventure University,

David J. May, Associate Vice President of Business Affairs, University of New Hampshire

David Hatton, AIA, Vice President, Stantec

Tom Ryder, Executive Director, Ancillary Services, retired, SUNY Oneonta

Gerald A. Tobin, Ph.D., Vice President for Student Life, Mercyhurst University

David Keala, Director of Food Services, BYU-Hawaii

Robert Rizzuto, Director of Dining Services, New York Institute of Technology

Todd Jutila, Director, University Food Services, Montana State University

Lori K. Helmer, Director of Dining Services, Auxiliary Enterprises, Ferris State University

Jeff Pauley, Sr. Director, Dining Services Spartan Shops, Inc., San Jose State University

Richard Fritz, Director of Residential Dining, Northern Illinois University

Dr. Leif Hartmark, Vice President for Finance and Administration, retired, SUNY Oneonta

Cindy Atkins, Director of Dining and Conference Service, St. Lawrence University

Tom Larsen, Founder and Owner, Pillar House Restaurant

Alexandra Marie, my oldest daughter, thank you for making the final decision for the picture we used for the cover of the book. More importantly, thank you for my first granddaughter, Riley Marie, that, at almost two months young, has warmed my heart in ways I did not think possible.

Madison Virginia, my youngest daughter, you inspire me every day with your love and support and your competitive spirit to succeed and your uncanny ability to advise me on my selection of one of my most commented on competitive professional advantages, my colorful collection of ties.

Chris Brown, my personal trainer, has worked with me for the past 8 years. Chris has made it easy to be and stay fit in spite of the rigors and pressures of our world today and the unforgiving demands required to travel and run a business and serve our clients in the United States and Canada.

Paul McDonald, Richard Gray, David Small and Keith St. Onge, in my opinion are four of the world's best barefoot waterskiing instructors. Keith and David are reigning barefoot waterskiing world champions. Your training, friendship, inspiration and patience has not only made me an acceptable barefoot water-skier, but you all have taught me life lessons that permit me to soar to heights, physically, spiritually and professionally, ten years ago, I would have thought impossible.

Don Boudreau has been a very close friend for almost 25 years. Don, you have inspired me as a person and as an entrepreneur. You spent seven years captaining your 38 foot sail boat around the world with your wonderful wife Carol, and then you returned home and came out of retirement to start your exotic wood handcrafted box business that is now flourishing.

Ron Sinclair, your spirit guides me every day.

Without the support of these individuals, the love and support of my brothers, John and Cameron and sister Nancy and their families and a host of others, I would not be in a position today to write this book or claim any modicum of success. This is my village.

CHAPTER ONE

Where Does It Hurt?

ON A SCALE OF one to ten, how much pain are you experiencing with your campus dining program? In your professional gut, do you feel like your dining program should offer more, but at the same time question whether or not your school can afford it? Or maybe you've decided that the program is great, and yet receive complaints because students have unused meals or dining dollars every week.

Are you struggling with a host of issues concerning the labor force, health safety, and deferred maintenance? Are your dining facilities state-of-the-art, 1970s' venues, but your capital construction plan has a list of higher priority construction projects ahead of a much-needed dining facility facelift?

Are you suffering silently, or is the chatter of nagging complaints from administrators, students, and family mounting?

How is your recruitment? Is it growing, or is it suffering because Admissions steers prospective students away from outdated dining facilities? Are your retention rates where you want them to be, or is there room for improvement? Are your alumni less than passionate about providing your school with ongoing support?

At first, these factors may seem unrelated, but in my forty years of experience in the food service industry, I have learned that the success of your dining program is integral to the success of your university. Everyone wants to feel connected, and there is no more powerful tool that creates a sense of community than an optimum dining program.

Your recruitment capture rates can increase when prospective students discover your premier dining venue that has a rich social energy. Your retention rates will increase because of a meaningful freshman experience that at its core has a socially rich dining experience for students to make and cement new friendships.

While they are dining and making new friends, the school has a once-in-a-lifetime opportunity to build brand loyalty. This is done not only through social energy, but also through the architecture, symbols, and legacy images that make up the interior design of the dining venue. These symbols embed themselves into the hearts and minds of the students as they see them two or three times each day throughout the academic year. These emotional connections and brand loyalty, or school spirit, are critical to a lifetime of good memories and alumnae loyalty and engagement.

So how do you get it right? To whom do you turn?

Most universities don't operate their own food services. Instead, they "contract out" the management of their dining departments to companies such as Aramark, Sodexo, and Chartwells to do it for them. These companies not only provide management services, but they also provide management advisory services.

It seems like a no-brainer. These food service operators will be champing at the bit for your business. They will pay a small fortune in desperately needed off-balance-sheet upfront capital in order to renovate those tired dining venues...Right?

They know the intricacies of college dining and they will implement a program to suit the unique needs of your campus...Right?

And of course, they will put the unique needs of your campus ahead of the fiduciary responsibility they have to their stockholders. And, without an independent appraisal from any other legitimate source, the contractor will offer you in capital investment what your program is truly worth...Right?

After they wow you with the branded and non-branded possibilities, promises of a partnership gives you comfort that they will work out all of the details after you sign their contract and all of your problems will be solved...Right?

WRONG. At this point, a little alarm should be sounding, "Danger, Will Robinson!"

Essentially there are two forms of management you can use to manage your dining program: self-operated, or contracted-out.

It is my professional opinion that a self-operated dining department is the optimum form of management a school can rely on. And I'll tell you why.

For most universities that contract out, this food service provider that will control tens of millions of dollars of food and non-food purchases for their school is also the sole source of advice and guidance as to how the school should make decisions in all of these areas. No matter how you slice it (no pun intended), there is a blatant conflict of interest.

Remember, the operator's fiduciary responsibility is to its stockholders, not you or your school. That's not to say that all operators are bad. On the contrary, I believe there are many good operators that can provide management services. But there is no operator that can provide good management services *in addition to* consulting services.

The problem is that most of these companies don't pay the university the attention it requires to understand the unique cultural, philosophic, and geographic needs and translate those into a dining program that not just meets, but exceeds those needs.

These operators are not social architects. Nor are the team members that they select to run your program. It is rare that the general manager selected by the operator and placed on your campus was involved in the development of the bid. And once the contract is signed and the extremely impressive team of executives, trainers, and marketers with their PowerPoint presentations go away, you are left with the strengths and weaknesses of one general manager to run your dining program. But the ones who selected the general manager simply didn't spend time on campus to determine what the program should be. They don't get to know the unique culture and community of the university and what it stands for.

These operators present a portfolio illustrating what they're capable of doing. It's impressive information, but during the presentation there's rarely a correlation between the actual cost of what they are capable of doing and the terms of the contract at it applies to your campus.

Not to mention, many of the small, but important, details such as hours of operation and menu pricing, will be worked out later. As far as hours of operation go, they proffer that it will be worked out based on "mutually agreeable" terms after the contract is signed. As for operating days for each of these locations, it will be based on "mutually agreeable" terms, after the contract is signed as well.

This leaves universities at a disadvantage because once the contract is signed, the school no longer has any leverage in the negotiation. That means that if you'd like to make a change to the hours of operation, the contractor has the power to demand a certain amount of dollars in order to do so. If you don't have the money to do it, then you're out of luck until the contract is up. More often than not, the students end up getting the short end of that stick programmatically.

In essence, the school has lost their ability to create or modify the program without being taken advantage of financially after the contract has been signed.

The consequence isn't just students missing a meal because they couldn't make the hours of operation work with their schedule. The problem goes beyond the need to provide the necessary caloric intake for students.

As I mentioned before, the strength of your dining program, both in terms of quality and atmosphere and access, strongly contributes to or detracts from the social architecture and the success of your students at your university. But who wants to engage in a program where the food is less than delicious, the meal plan is antagonistic, and the environment is all but unwelcoming?

The reality is that if the program is not optimum after you've signed the contract, you'll have to either write a large check to opt out of the agreement, or be stuck with a mediocre program for the remaining term of the agreement.

That upfront capital that initially enticed you into signing the contract is now a hostage fee. This can effectively memorialize the status quo.

So how do you ensure that your program is the optimum package that will create the greatest value as it relates to recruitment, retention, and long-term alumni relations? How do you avoid leaving millions on the table and getting stuck with a subpar dining program?

That is precisely where I step in as a campus planner for dining services and a social architect for your campus.

Through my extensive experience working with colleges and universities, I've learned the right questions to ask and who to ask. Is the dining program bringing students together socially? Is it enriching their social experience? Is it creating a meaningful freshman experience? Is it adding to the quality of residential life? Is the dining program perceived as an amenity to students, as opposed to a financial albatross?

My team does the research so that we can answer these questions before the first brick is laid. We're going to come to your campus and determine the optimum dining program in terms of location, hours of operation, menu variety and selection, methods of service, meal plans, operating days per year, and levels of catering.

On top of that, we're going to determine how to get the maximum number of students to participate in residential dining and retail dining on your campus by creating your optimum program.

In *Star Wars*, Yoda says "May the force be with you." The power of campus dining goes along with this concept. I believe there is a Force in all of us, whether it is social or spiritual. With my skills, professional intuition, and team of professionals, we are able to create a program and align the dynamics of that program so that it directly connects to this spiritual and social force. It creates what I like to call a "gravitational pull" into the dining venues.

This social gravitational force is evident at Starbucks, Whole Foods Markets, and even your own local venue that you frequent. The point is that you don't go there because you *have to*. You go there because you *want to*. You can apply the same concept to an optimum dining program. Students don't eat there because they are *forced to* due to a meal plan requirement. They *choose* to eat there and return voluntarily because they want to. They look forward to seeing their friends and experiencing the social energy generated in these venues.

So what is more important: the food, or the social energy and fellowship of a class? The beauty of what my team does is that you don't have to choose. Because one feeds the other, and we will find an optimum program that uses food as a catalyst for building community. It's a profound win-win-win for the campus community, university, and yes—even the operator.

There is an enormous level of specificity and detail involved, and everything is spelled out in the Request for Proposal (RFP) to solicit bids from food service operators that we will put together. Once my team has worked with the university to create the optimum dining program, we will act as your independent agent and facilitate the entire RFP operator selection process.

One of the tenets of a successful negotiation for what in some cases could easily be a contract valued at 100 to 700 million dollars for your university is to not have the individuals negotiating the contract be the final decision makers. We are the "tip of the spear" and act solely on your behalf with your directives throughout the process.

My process is unique. We do not ask the potential

bidders to propose a dining program from the shelves of their archives for your campus. I will have conducted a thorough process of discovery and production of actionable recommendations, reviewed and approved by you, that will meet the unique cultural, social, philosophic, and financial objectives of your campus.

When my team develops a request for proposal there is little or no ambiguity regarding the programs, hours of operation, menu variety and selection, operating days, meal plans, mix of national brands, pricing, management structure, financial requirements, capital, commissions, overrides, etc.

Buddha says, "If you don't go within you go without." I will go within your culture and campus to develop this program that is uniquely you. At the same time, we do not want to in any way stifle the food service operator's creativity. So we encourage bidders to provide alternate bids if they feel there is a better approach to developing your dining program.

The difference is that instead of asking, "What do we need?" you're telling them, "This is what we need. This is the best plan for our campus."

With our method, there is no conflict of interest. The bidders don't have to figure it out for the campus, and the university can rest assured knowing they are getting an optimum program because we've already determined exactly what that is.

We've written the RFP with a huge level of detail. Nothing is based on mutually agreeable terms after the fact. Everything is spelled out in detail for every business unit in each business segment for every year of the term of the contract. As part of the program development, we will effectively appraise and value your dining program in order to independently establish what your program is worth to your school in commissions, or overrides, and off-balance-sheet capital dollars. We have independently established the financial terms and dollar value of your agreement. The financial goals have been set.

I do this job not only because it is something I know and understand, but also because there is nothing that I'm more passionate about. When I walk on and immerse myself in your campus and interact with the students and venues, I can not only see, but—as corny as this sounds—I can *feel* the potential. And I will do everything in my power to ensure that social and dining potential is realized.

I was recently part of a team brought on to build a dining hall as part of a new freshman residential complex. My job was to work with the architect to determine the best layout and design of the dining hall that would lead to an optimum dining experience.

I had lots of questions going into the project. Should it be all-you-care-to-eat or à la carte? Should we sell national brands like Taco Bell, or should it be a more traditional residential program? What should the hours of operation be?

I soon ran into a problem. This was going to be a fast-track project, and the university wanted to break ground before all of the appropriate research was in. My concern was that if they created the freshman dining hall in a vacuum, then there would be a large margin for error.

How awful would it be if the following fall, after the building is up, we do a study and realize that if we had only designed it a little differently, it would have made a huge difference in terms of the added value of the campus-wide dining program?

I learned that the plan on the table had a three hundred-seat dining hall with at least fifty percent retail and limited food service. From my experience, I knew that the plan was probably not the optimum setup to serve freshman students. And I knew that with just a little more research, we could knock the design out of the park, and see the results to back it up. The results being a meaningful socially rich experience for freshmen built around a dining program with unsurpassed levels of student participation. Thus, contributing to a financially viable dining program increased recruitment and retention rates for the campus.

I went to the Director of Auxiliary Services and said, "I can be there next Tuesday. If you give me one day on campus, I can go around, conduct interviews, and create a high-level vision statement outlining your optimum dining program."

He called me back on Monday and said, "Okay, come on down."

I flew out on Monday, conducted research on Tuesday, and on Wednesday was in the Vice President's office with my results.

I was faced with an arduous task: what I saw as an opportunity to transform their dining program and social architecture of their campus was different from the plan that was already set out. My vision embraced and supported the President's vision of further evolving their campus into a destination with high levels of student engagement, but the details of our vision completely contradicted the plan that the boss had already set in stone. I had to move quickly with passion, conviction, and evidence to get their campus what it needed.

I saw the freshman dining hall as an experience that could be open from seven in the morning until midnight, seven days a week. It would be an amazing place for students to get all of their meals, every day. They could come all day and all night. They could come in groups and they could study, socialize, eat, or snack. What better way to introduce all of these freshman students to their new home, and to meet their new away-from-home family?

I had learned from my research that the venue on

the opposite side of campus, where all the students currently went, was inconvenient and unpopular. I could see transforming that into a twenty-four-hour operation with unlimited meal plans and amplifying the social force of attraction by adding soft seating, computer terminals, games, and lounge space twenty-four hours a day. Students would pay one price for the meal plan, and they would have the option, just like a health club membership, as to how many times they use the dining hall.

I saw that instead of just shifting business from one location to the new location, we could create a meaningful freshman experience, and on the other side of campus create a meaningful experience for upperclassmen, living on and in off-campus apartments, in a different way. This would not only benefit recruitment because of the impression these changes would make, but it would increase sales as well. And it would improve retention from first to second year because of the social connection.

The boss didn't like what I had to say. He wanted limited options and retail so as to not draw students away from the other venue—end of story. He saw this addition as a supplement to the one across campus, not a replacement. The students could pile their tray as high as they like with salad or soup, à la carte. If they wanted to sit down and have a big meal, they could walk all the way to the other side of campus to get it.

When I left the room, I could tell that the Vice President was not happy. After all, this man was almost seventy years old, unbelievably smart, and had been making most of the financial decisions on campus for years. Nobody had ever walked into his office and so passionately disagreed with him, not to mention tell him a different approach could better serve the University.

I was brought back the next week for the architect's meeting, and the boss announced that he was ready to make a decision. He said, "I want fifty percent retail," and then he looked over at me and began to explain how he believed it would work.

And with a room full of people—the architects and decision makers—I knew that if I didn't stop the train now, it was gone. The school would miss a huge opportunity.

I couldn't let this happen.

"Sir," I said, "with all due respect, I think you have it backwards." You could have heard a pin drop, the room was so silent. "In fact," I continued, "I'll bet my fee on this. If what I produce as a result of this isn't in the best interest of your campus in moving it forward, I will sacrifice my professional fee."

I was trying so hard to make my point and suggest that I was not doing this to enrich myself, but to better the university, that I actually wagered my own compensation.

That got their attention. The next day the VP called me into his office. Just as I was beginning to explain that I can often get passionate and speak out, he interrupted me. "David," he said, "you stopped a train. You did the right thing."

I had heard stories that this man holds very strong opinions, and when he believes he's being sold a pig in a poke does not hesitate to abruptly tell people to leave the room in front of an entire board of people. But this time, he didn't do that. He was finally able to see my vision, which put his students first, through the detailed report my team and I pulled together, and through the passion and conviction I displayed unlike any consultant before.

I believe that there is no other food service manager working for a contractor who will step out and say what I did for no other reason than to serve the interests of your school. Even if they saw the opportunity, they would probably stay silent because the company would slap them down.

This ability to see what others don't see, combined with my passion and conviction to get it right for our clients, makes a big difference when it comes to attaining goals, especially in food services where the optimum program is based upon complex layers. But

I think it all comes down to one question: What is the value of your program?

We'll figure that out for you. We'll tell you what you deserve. We'll tell you what that program should look like. And I'm going to walk you through that process, as well as all the other factors to consider, in the following chapters. In addition, you can visit my website at www.porterkhouwconsulting.com

So I'll ask you again: Where does it hurt? On a scale of one-to-ten, what is your level of pain? Have you had enough? Are you willing to step up to the plate, take responsibility for your situation, and ask for the professional help necessary that will put you and your university first?

Your answer to these questions will influence the success of every student that matriculates to your campus. Not only that, but it can be worth millions to your school.

Chapter Two

Great School, But the Food Sucks

CAMPUS DINING IS ABOUT creating a program that not only enhances campus life, but will also help your university grow and expand.

But if you want to know the most powerful ways in which an optimum dining program will affect your college, then it all comes down to the three R's: Recruitment, Retention, and alumni Relations.

Years ago, students had limited options in terms of their education. If they were lucky enough to afford college, it often meant the local university. But now the game has changed. Not only do they have more options, but students are also bombarded with emails, postcards, and campus representatives recruiting them to attend their university.

It's as if colleges are engaged in an arms race to outshine their opponents by whatever means necessary.

And what's the number one non-academic ammo to have in your recruitment artillery? A stellar dining program.

During a consultation, one of the first questions I ask a Director of Admissions is, "Do you steer your prospective families to the dining hall (if it's a residential college) or retail dining venues (if it's a commuter campus), or do you steer them away from the dining facilities?"

Their answer to my question provides me with important insight as to whether or not their dining program is "ready for prime time"—or ready to host the thousands of students, faculty, staff, and visitors who will come through on a daily basis.

Universally, my clients will say that they want their dining facilities to be a memorable experience on the campus tour. They know that a student's first impression of the dining hall could be a tipping point for whether or not they commit to their institution. After all, this place will be their home for at least the next year, and they want to make sure their home is a place where they want to be.

But very rarely do they contemplate what "home" means to an incoming freshman.

For most of these students, home means a few bedrooms, a living room, a family space, and—most importantly—a kitchen. Why is the kitchen most important? In a majority of households, the kitchen serves as the social vortex where family and friends gather around to dine and socialize. Apple pie, hot dogs, breakfast cereal, mom—what's the common denominator? The kitchen.

The kitchen is a non-negotiable element in creating a home. If a student who plans to live in the dorms comes on campus and sees that the dining hall is an uninviting ghost town and the kitchen's food is drab, then it's not going to feel like home and they certainly won't want to live there. Even if the rest of the campus is pristine, outdated dining halls can cast a dark shadow on your university's image.

This leads me to the next question that I ask the Director of Housing: "Does, dining contribute to, or detract from, what you want to accomplish with your housing program?" I recently completed a project with my team where the school had documented that the number one reason that freshman students moved out of on-campus housing was because of the current state of their dining program and policies.

You want to create an atmosphere and experience that draws students in. The dining hall must serve two purposes: practical (delivering daily caloric needs), and social (creating an environment to meet and spend time with friends). So it's an integral part of daily life—if you get it right. And if you get it right, then the success trickles down to admissions, housing, student life, advancement, and alumni relations.

Details such as lighting, finishes, seating, display cooking stations—they all play a role in creating this atmosphere. Just imagine walking into a campus dining hall that is filled with students eating, talking, and socializing. In baseball parlance, this is the "big game." It's an exciting atmosphere where students can see and be seen. Now contrast that to a subpar dining hall that no one wants to use. It's empty and isolating, and that's the impression that students will walk away with.

Regardless of your flashy brochures and top-notch academic programs, those dining facilities could keep your recruitment numbers in the doldrums.

But what about retention—the percentage of students who are not washed out due to poor academic performance or financial insolvency and return to your school as sophomores? What about the students who do enroll? Once you get them on your campus, you want to keep them there and have them graduate from your school. The way in which your dining program is organized can be your greatest asset to increase retention or your biggest ball and chain keeping you stuck far below expectations.

On a residential campus, there can be anywhere from a few hundred to many thousands of students living in residence, in addition to the thousands of non-resident students living in apartments in close proximity. You have the opportunity to bring these students together and create a very powerful, socially rich, emotional experience that is unique to your institution. Dining can be the holy grail that brings students together and creates a unique meaningful experience that everyone wants to be a part of and impacts the success of your institution on every level as a student ascends through, and graduates from, your school.

But that's only if the campus-wide dining program is organized in the right way. Adversely, dining can work against you. It can be like a stink bomb if your dining program repels your students into their rooms and off-campus food establishments as they search for opportunities to dine and connect in ways that we all yearn for.

For example, I recently worked with a university that had three residential towers dedicated to freshman students. That's around nine hundred students living on-site! And what was their sole opportunity for social connection? The freshman dining commons—a glorified convenience store. No joke!

Students wanted to eat on campus, but what did they get? They got to wait in line to purchase a bag of chips, soda, or maybe some frozen food, and then take it back to their dorm to eat alone or with a few of their friends. For students on this campus, there was no dining facility. There was no meaningful social connector. But if the definition of a meaningful freshman social experience is bumping shoulders as you wait in line to pay, then mission accomplished.

I can tell you right away that this affects not only recruitment, but student retention as well. Making social connections (new friends) is essential and central to adapting to college life. But if you don't have the opportunity to connect with other students, then most likely you're going to have a miserable time and want to go elsewhere.

I interviewed a young lady at the campus who said to me, "We're homesick." She was a freshman at the time. "This is the first time we've been away from home. We want to go to a dining venue and be with our friends not only to eat, but to be able to talk and socialize."

Most administrators will acknowledge that the sooner students connect to each other socially, the more likely they are to return the following years. One administrator recently told me that the first thirty days for a freshman are the most important when it comes to making and establishing these social connections.

So I visited the President of this university and asked him about their retention rate. Initially, he gave me a very diplomatic answer. He said that they were doing pretty well in the mid-seventies, as compared to the other schools they had benchmarked. I knew this couldn't be the case because of the shadow cast by their inadequate dining hall.

I wanted to get to the root of the problem so that we could begin to think of solutions. So I said, "But sir, as President of this university, in terms of your own professional experience, in terms of what you believe should be an acceptable retention rate for this campus, how do you feel about the retention rate?"

He said, "It's unacceptable." It was in the mid-seventies, and he wanted it to be in the mid-eighties. I can tell you that when they adopt my vision for their campus, their retention rate will move significantly higher.

With the plan we laid out for their campus, these kids will come together socially, connect, make more friends, and have a more profound and meaningful common experience unique to this institution. They'll feel as though they're part of a larger group—the freshman class. And then they'll go on to be sophomores, and if the dining program is set up correctly, they'll continue to come together, even after they move to off-campus apartments as upperclassmen.

I can't emphasize it enough: by bringing students together, and using dining as the catalyst to do so, then not only does your recruitment rate go up, but it is profoundly powerful with increasing student retention rates as well.

This story is typical of most of the universities I work with. These universities always have the potential to increase recruitment and retention. After all, the students are already on campus. The only thing missing is the catalyst—the enriched uranium, if you will—to unleash the connecting force that is present in all of us, regardless of age.

The beauty of an optimum dining program is that it will not only allow your students to connect with each other, but with the school—or your "brand" as an institution of higher learning—as well.

Through the architecture or symbols in the dining room or building, whether they're pictures or legacy aspects of your campus, you can build your brand relationship with your students. By having these symbols in a location where they come and eat two or three times a day, every day, for their first year on campus, you can influence their school spirit and their lifetime loyalty as alumni to your institution in a huge way.

When it comes to dining options you make available to your students, I believe the school gets the first bite of the loyalty apple. It's not unlike Coke or Pepsi. These brands fight for the right to have exclusive beverage agreements on campus. They'll pay the school a premium so that all they sell on campus is their brand.

Coke and Pepsi know that some of the most impressionable years are between the ages of eighteen and twenty-three. During this period, people establish brand loyalties that can last a lifetime.

The Vice President on one of the campuses I worked with told me about an elderly woman who was in her eighties and had donated half a million dollars to the school, but only under strict conditions. Condition one: it had to be used in the cafeteria.

The school didn't want to use it in the cafeteria because they had other projects that they thought were more important. But she said she wouldn't give them the money unless they used it to upgrade the dining facilities.

After trying to convince her otherwise, they finally asked her why. And she replied, "Because over sixty years ago, under the clock in the cafeteria, I met my husband. My husband became very successful, and my life became what it was because of that meeting that day in the cafeteria under the clock."

This woman's story illustrates an important point: What makes a good alumni? Alumni spirit. What makes you want to contribute? The connection you have to a campus. If a student connects emotionally and the bond is made, then they will become a lifelong loyalist to that university.

My team capitalizes on honoring and capturing that social energy and coming up with clever ways to combine the student's innate need and desire to be social and make friends with the campus dining program.

We not only tell our clients what we think they're capable of, but we show them in diagrams and pictures and make a case. We show them that an opportunity not only exists on their campus, but there's a fairly inexpensive way to make that happen. We bring schematics, we bring examples, we bring revenue and expense projections—we bring everything we can to present to our client because we really want to open their mind to these possibilities. We present actionable step-by-step recommendations that will bring this new vision to life on their campus.

Your dining program could improve alumni relations, and could even increase enrollment. Because more students want to live on campus and be a part of that atmosphere, you may increase your housing occupancy and add significant value to the resident experience on your campus.

There are some campuses where they don't have enough beds. Other campuses where they have ten to fifteen percent of their beds empty and they're trying to figure out how to make their students want to live on campus longer. Dining is the answer.

The point of this arms race—the new buildings, the first-class housing on campus, the magnificent student centers, recreation centers, dining halls, architecture, and manicured landscapes—is to win the war of bringing students to your campus and keeping them there.

In terms of the three all-important R's—Recruitment, Retention and alumni Relations—there is nothing more profoundly powerful, especially for freshmen, than bringing people together socially to optimize that social connectivity.

And that is achieved through an organized, developed, and properly rolled-out dining plan. And I can do that for you. In the words sung by Carly Simon, "Nobody does it better/ makes me feel sad for the rest."

God has bestowed each of us with certain gifts. It's hard to explain, but I see things that others just don't see. This is my gift. I love what I do with the support of my dream team, and I do it with a passion second to none.

I can't claim that these are revolutionary ideas. Indeed, the importance of an optimum dining program is known to most decision makers on campus. However, it's such a complicated issue that most people don't know where to begin or who to go to for independent, unbiased guidance in order to change their dining program for the better.

I can, and will, do that for you. In order to do so, let's consider the relationship between the school and the vendor as a marriage.

In an ideal partnership, both parties look out for

each other. They want what is best, and will do what it takes to achieve that.

And, like a marriage, everyone knows when a partnership has gone south. One side is dissatisfied, one side's needs are going unaddressed, and someone is very unhappy. But ending the partnership is easier said than done. Oftentimes one will discover they're hanging on without really knowing why.

Many of the dining services' contracts I encounter are like a bad marriage. In some extreme cases, it is almost the same as the battered spouse syndrome.

But what makes this marriage between a college and a food management company unique is that most people in charge of their university's food program aren't aware that it's bad, or if they do, they don't believe they can do or deserve a world-class dining program.

They know that something needs to change: students are protesting because there's an insect problem in the cafeteria; the President is pressuring them to reduce complaints from parents; the Director of Housing says meal plans are the reason why students don't want to live on campus; Student Life says students should be able to spend their dining dollars off-campus; and Admissions is doing everything in its power to keep students away from the cafeteria so as to not make a bad first impression.

Little do they know that this Pandora's box of problems is because of a complete lack of vision and a failed partnership.

Food service operations are extraordinarily complex. You've got labor issues, health safety issues, facility issues, equipment issues, student satisfaction, revenue, and expense issues. You could have an MBA from Harvard, or be a financial wizard, but you just can't get your head around it.

When it's bad, it's a political nightmare. You've got parents calling, kids calling, and you just want it to go away.

So you decide to rebid the contract.

It is at this strategic moment that the food companies will return with open arms.

They want your business, so they'll tell you everything you want to hear: "We love you, we'll take care of you, we'll do right by you."

And on top of that, they'll write you a check for a million bucks, if only you commit to a long-term agreement.

Sometimes they'll even fly you out on their private jet to check out their other venues. They'll wine you, dine you, play a lot of golf with you, and do everything in their power to seduce you.

So what do you do?

You sign on the dotted line.

But the devil is in the details. Did this company spend time getting to know your university? Is their offering based on the needs of your school? Furthermore, does your contract ensure that you will receive what is best for your school? More often than not, the answer to both is no.

This leaves you with a contract that has holes so big these companies could drive an eighteen-wheeler truck through—and they do.

You find yourself back in the same boat, with the same complaints, and the same mountain of problems. It's time for round two: campus versus company. And let me tell you, I'm not betting on the former.

But it's not your fault.

Why? Because you don't know what you don't know.

You don't know that these companies who purport to have your best interests at heart are really more concerned with their own profit. They'll make up excuses as to why they can't keep your dining halls open longer, or why they can't offer this particular menu—which your school really needs—and why they can't get you the best general manager or executive chef when really it all comes down to profit. Or my favorite is when they sit across the table from you and attempt to put the burden on you to tell them what to do. Then when you tell them what you want programmatically, you are presented with numerous "Hobson's choices" that nine times out of ten will stop you dead in your tracks.

In typical business situations, both parties have been there before.

Both parties have adequate representation.

It's nobody's first rodeo.

But dining services is a very different brand of negotiation because one side has all the experience. It's impossible to have any insight unless you've been making these deals for decades.

In almost any other type of business, there are people lining up to represent you and ensure you get your fair share. Take the car insurance business, for example. How many times have you seen lawyers on TV barking at you: "Let us get what you deserve. DON'T AGREE TO ANYTHING. Call us and we'll represent you and look out for your best interests!"

People aren't lining up to provide that service for campus dining programs. But if they were, I'd be at the head of the queue.

What David Boies is to his clients, I will be that for you. I can help you not only end a bad marriage, but quite possibly save it and make it stronger than ever. I will conduct a unique process from developing a new vision to securing a fully-executed agreement that will give you your ideal program. I will ensure you have the tools and knowledge so that you will never be neglected again.

I receive a lot of phone calls from administrators across the country who are at the end of their rope. So I'll come on campus, immerse myself in their community both on and off campus, and with the support of my team do what no other consultant in North America can do better—collect the data, get to know the value of their campus, and produce the optimum vision for their social architecture through a properly organized dining program.

My vision will transform the social landscape of your campus in ways you may never have considered and produce the social engagement results you have yearned for, but could never achieve.

There is nothing more exciting for me than discovering the potential to completely transform the social landscape of campus life. And I present my findings to the administrator with the same passion.

But this passion is not always returned. In fact, it's often met with a good deal of skepticism. After years of working with these companies, it's difficult for some administrators to realize that things should, and can be, different/better.

They are returning to that flawed strategy. Instead of first asking, "What do we want?" they're asking, "What do you think we can get?" And as a result, they get even less than they think they can get.

For example, when I was developing a new program with the campus Director of Housing, I asked,

"In a perfect world, what kind of hours of operation would you have?"

He replied, "Well, I'd like it open later, but it's just not realistic from a labor perspective." It can become very strange. All of a sudden, the administrators who are the most dissatisfied with the current operator/program, unwittingly become defenders of the status quo.

I replied, "Just for a minute, don't even consider the labor issues. Don't consider finances. Don't consider what it'll cost to either do it or not do it. Don't consider whether the operator is capable of doing it or not. We'll do that for you. Let's just talk about your campus and your students for a minute. What do the students want? When do they want it? Where do they go?"

Finally he opened up: "Well, in that case, we want it open twenty-four hours a day. We'd like to have unlimited coffee. We'd like the students to be able to come in there at one o'clock in the morning and study, or at ten at night and get a meal."

That was exactly the information I needed, because it was what the school really needed.

But again, these administrators are still very skeptical because of years spent working with food management companies who intentionally or unintentionally had led their clients to believe that none of these programmatic options were viable for their students on their campus.

It's like the Stockholm Syndrome—you've been taken hostage and your only sense of safety comes from falling in love with, and defending, the people who kidnapped you. Universities get so accustomed to this poor treatment that it becomes the norm. And so when I deliver a new program to the school administrators, they are uneasy because they think the operator will shut them down or abandon them. Or more importantly, their food service operator has convinced them that they are the authority on college and university dining programs, and if they have not been able to solve our problems and deliver a world-class dining program, who in the world does David Porter think he is...?

They say, "The operator can't afford that. It's not realistic to pay the operator that kind of money. We have union workers here and there's no way we can staff that late at night."

Which is why I say, "Let's determine what your program should be for your campus, and then we will structure that in a way so that we will get bids to buy in on that business."

Once all the bids come in, we'll determine if, in fact, it is too expensive. And then we'll do a little horse-trading in the eleventh hour with our finalists. We'll make adjustments to the hours, tweak this, tweak that. Above all, we start with what we want first, and then start giving it away in the end if we need to.

My colleague did a pre-bid call the other day for a college in Virginia. They didn't know if anybody would show up because of the bold new dining program spelled out in the RFP that in fact would get their school exactly what their students needed. The school thought it was too radical.

We had eleven companies at the pre-bid conference.

Another time I was at a wealthy campus that had been doing fifteen million dollars of business per year. The VP asked, "Do you think anybody will come to the pre-bid conference?"

He had thirteen companies at the pre-bid conference!

The list goes on.

Sometimes the only true way for administrators to determine the legitimacy of our program from an operator's perspective—beyond what we tell them is legitimate—is to let me and my team develop an RFP, and then let a half-dozen contractors bid on it.

As a result of that bidding process, they'll not only say what they can or can't do (and I can assure you there will be a lot more "cans" than "can'ts" in those responses), we'll also find out what it's worth in the open market.

But the difference is, we're going to tell them what we think it's worth, and they're going to have a goal-post to shoot for.

I've read a lot of books about being successful, and

every author will tell you that it's about setting goals and knowing where you want to go. Most administrators have a distorted view of where they want to go because of their bad marriage and diminished expectations with food service operating companies.

They simply don't know what they don't know. What they do know is that they want to make it better and eliminate the negatives. But they don't really know what the endgame looks like.

They don't know how to independently appraise and/or value their dining services. If they're offered $500,000, should it be a million, or is that right? If they're offered three million, should it be six million? If you had a piece of jewelry or an antique painting, would you just take the buyer's word as to what it was worth, or would you get it appraised first? We all know the answer. And if you did not get it appraised, you would probably be embarrassed to ever admit that minor fact to any of your friends after the sale went through and you realized you got way less than what you deserved.

However, in the contracted dining realm, the convention is to not spend a dime to independently evaluate and appraise a dining program that could be worth tens or hundreds of millions of dollars over the term of an agreement. Instead, they let the buyer (in this case the food service management company), who has virtually nothing to lose and everything to gain in this completely lopsided negotiation, tell them what to do and what it is worth. As Amy and Seth say in one of their "Weekend Update" bits on *Saturday Night Live,* "REALLY?" "REALLY?"

You would spend more to independently appraise a $5,000 diamond than a fifty-million-dollar dining program? "REALLY?"

They don't know how to value the program financially or in terms of what the program should be for the campus. They don't know the inner mechanics of the food service operations, so they don't know how to keep people in check. Is the charge for a service legitimate? Is it comparable to the industry averages? Should they be responsible for paying these charges or not?

They provide the management services, but what do you provide? You provide the campus, the building, the food venues, and the equipment. In most cases you provide the utilities. Sometimes they don't even have to pay rent or commissions.

You provide a captive student population, and if your campus is residential with mandatory meal plans, you provide a one hundred percent guaranteed revenue base, but, you're not getting an equal return on investment, and your dining program is terrible.

And that's when a partnership becomes a bad marriage.

If you don't know the value of your dining program, and if you don't know the endgame, then you'll carry on in this bad relationship. But again, the formula for a good program is so complex, it's no wonder that many of these administrators are going back to these companies.

It's like going to med school: I don't know how to operate on my knee, but if I went to med school, I might know.

Administrators earned their position because they are accomplished and well educated, but they don't know how to operate or to get the desired results from their dining services because of the complexities and the built-in conflicts of interest that saddle food service management companies.

I've been going to med school and honing my craft for the past forty-one years.

We know your school is unique. You're culturally unique, the philosophy of your campus is unique, and you're geographically unique.

In order to create your optimum dining program, it is essential to know: Where do the students live? How do the commuters get to campus? Where do they park their cars? Where do they get off the bus? Where's the academic core of the campus? Where do the students go to class on campus? Where are the dining venues in terms of that activity? And what is your goal in terms of creating a social connection on campus? Is dining contributing to that, or detracting?

These are the questions that operators fail to ask, and as a result, you end up in a bad marriage.

I've been on so many campuses, and I can tell you that they're all extremely different in terms of their students, eating habits, geographic layout, culture, mix of resident and non-resident students, and other factors. It's our goal to determine, culturally, who you are or what you are, and then what role does food or dining services play to further that cause?

Our company will reinvent your dining program.

We're not just moving around deck chairs on the Titanic; we're changing everything. But we're doing it in a way that lines it up with who you are as a campus, and what you want to accomplish.

This is just phase one: End your bad marriage.

Forget about the contract, the operators, the people who help you run it. The first order of business is discovering who you are and what your program should be to enrich and optimize the social and dining experience for your students. So let's focus on that next.

CHAPTER THREE

Forty Years in the Making

I'VE TALKED A LOT about my beliefs for your campus. I've gone on and on about enhancing your campus through the most fundamental building block you have—your dining program.

But what makes me the authority on this matter? Aside from my passion and conviction, what are my credentials that prove that I not only talk the talk, but walk the walk? Furthermore, why am I able to see the opportunities on campus when other highly intelligent and capable directors and advisors have not?

History influences both the present and future, and my history is such that when I look back on my life, I can see that I was meant for this job. More than that, I've created this niche for myself.

I grew up in Wellesley, Massachusetts, and my very first work experience, after the obligatory paper route, was in 1972 washing pots and mopping floors in the kitchen of a restaurant nearby in Newton called the Pillar House. This wasn't your run-of-the-mill New England restaurant. Pillar House was a fine dining establishment, complete with white tablecloths, silverware, tuxedoed servers, and a firm "jacket required" policy. People came to this place to indulge in top-notch cuisine and have the total luxury experience, to boot. And I loved giving it to them.

I loved providing an unforgettable experience for the diners. I loved it so much, in fact, that I worked my way through every position that restaurant had to fill. I washed pots, I mopped floors, I grilled meat, I baked, I bartended, I served—I did everything, all the way up to being assistant to the owner. The owner of the Pillar House quickly became my mentor. He was a visionary in the restaurant business and was often mocked by the public when he implemented concepts that at the time seemed foolhardy, yet in the end allowed his business to flourish. He closed the restaurant on Saturday, the busiest night of the week, to allow his staff some time off to improve their quality of life. He invited guests to take a tour of the kitchen. He was one of the first restaurants in the United States to ban smoking.

Many predicted he would soon go out of business. In fact, his business increased dramatically over time. He is one of a kind, a visionary many years ahead of his time, and never took no for an answer. I was his employee, student, number one fan, and to this day proud and blessed to be his friend.

When I graduated from the School of Hotel, Restaurant and Institutional Management at Michigan State University in 1979, it seemed only natural that I continue on this course. My parents couldn't have been happier. In truth, my love for dining is a family thing. My father was an electrical engineer, but he had always wanted the entrepreneurial experience of running a business. So when I graduated from Michigan State, he bought a restaurant space for me back home in downtown Boston and we went into business together.

Here I was, a twenty-one-year-old kid running my own restaurant. I didn't know what I didn't know, and boy did I love it! Passion, unrelenting work ethic, not taking no for an answer, and customer service just came naturally to me. I lived for the challenge of figuring out what our guests wanted, how to get repeat customers, how to optimize the dining experience, and how to create value. These were all things that I had studied and practiced with my restaurant job and college education. Now all that experience was paying off.

I decided that it was time to take the next step in my career. I was ready for a challenge, and so I made my first foray into higher education dining.

I went to work for Harvard University in 1988 in

their self-operated dining services. But it wasn't long before one of my professors from Michigan State called me up and asked me to work for his consulting firm. Again, I was always up for a challenge, so I jumped at the opportunity to move to Annapolis, Maryland and try something new.

I eventually moved on to work for one of the biggest food service management consulting and design firms in the world. And it was here that I continued to develop a unique process of discovery that would become the centerpiece of my approach to uncover unique opportunities for each of my clients. By implementing this discovery process, I could gather enough information to understand the unique needs of each client so that when it came time to make recommendations I could, with complete conviction, put my reputation on the line knowing that what we presented was in the best interest of the institution.

One of the most important lessons I learned was the value of qualitative (face-to-face) market research, rather than just relying on guesswork or intuition or the prevailing conventional wisdom that's bantered about at conferences and in trade publications. The best data, or as I like to refer to it, "golden nuggets," comes from interacting with the very people who will use the product you offer. As I've mentioned, the extent to which my team and I become immersed in the campus community is a rare approach in the food consulting business, but it is a make or break move for the success of any given program—including my company.

The other thing I learned about contracted food service programs is that it is enormously difficult for a layperson to break down and understand the legitimacy of financial statements produced by contractors. One of the first projects I had when I got into the consulting business back in 1990 was for a university in the Mid-Atlantic region. The account was doing close to $6 million per year, and the contractor was sustaining close to $100,000 per year in losses that were subsidized by the university.

I was asked to review the contract. I approached these reviews with professional respect and an equal dose of contempt for these multibillion-dollar multinational food service management corporations. With my experience in the restaurant industry, I was able to pinpoint gray areas that were costing the school money, but making solid returns for the operators. All in all, when I looked at the financial report, I saw that this college was losing around $100,000 each year with their food service contract.

This was no secret, but for these people who didn't have as much experience with operations, it was difficult to understand why they were losing so much money. For them, the fact that their operator was taking over a million dollars each year and still crying poor mouth didn't stick out like a sore thumb.

When I looked at the different line item expenses and how they were coded, and compared those to the world of the restaurant business, the expenses just didn't make sense. With that knowledge, I was able to fill the gap that others had left. I was able to bring to the table not only an understanding of what creates an optimum dining experience, but also what makes the clock tick, financially.

I continued to work and learn from this company until I once again reached those crossroads where I realized that I was ready for the next great challenge. I asked myself, what could be more challenging than moving up the corporate ladder? Creating your own corporation, of course.

I decided to start my own company. It was a huge leap of faith. I didn't burn any bridges with my former employers, and I left without any work offers or secret handshakes from former or existing clients. I was completely on my own, and I had to start from the ground up—literally.

My office was headquartered in the basement of my home. Every day, I would wake up, put on a suit and tie, and walk down to my basement to do work. This was before businesses used email, so my work was all about putting on a smile, cold calling, visiting campuses, and sending out mass mailings announcing my business.

I soon realized that there were far more challenges to starting a new business than I had initially believed. There were the long hours where my day started at four a.m. and usually didn't end until midnight, six days a week. To make the most of my time, I would dictate proposals and reports on all of the clients I met with, and I desperately needed a transcriptionist to transcribe the tapes into WordPerfect. I remember calling the local temp agency and requesting a typist who was proficient in WordPerfect, which was the program I used. When the operator got around to asking about my business and I informed her that I operated out of my basement, she basically told me to take a hike and would not send anyone.

Eventually, I just left out the part about my location and finally a temp agency sent over a typist. I later learned, however, that she spent about half an hour sitting in the driveway, trying to decide if the person inside was a total nutcase. Luckily, she took a chance and ended up working with me for the next two years.

Despite the experience and skills I had to offer, I believed there was a definite stigma against start-ups like my own. The last thing I wanted was for people to have a poor impression before they even got to know my business, so it did not take long before I renamed my company Porter Consulting Worldwide. On my business cards, instead of just listing my home address, I added a suite number to look more professional, as if we were in an office building. And even though everyone said I only needed one phone line for calls and fax, I ordered two separate phone numbers and promoted that on my business cards. But maybe most importantly, I insisted that a real person answer the phone every time instead of using a voice mail phone attendant. This was all to provide a high level of professionalism and service to my prospects and clients. And it worked!

Those first couple of months, my business plan consisted of a paper napkin with the following scribbled on the back: "Sign at least $10,000 worth of business over the next two months or throw in the towel and go to work for someone else. Oh, and retire in twenty-five years."

Well, I ended up signing over $40,000 worth of business. Not to mention, I felt like I was finally in my groove. I had a diligent routine, and I was working harder than ever before and I loved it.

I would wake up at four in the morning, go downstairs, and dictate reports. In the afternoon, I would make cold calls and visit potential clients, and at night I'd go home and write up reports for the people I had met with. I would do this five or six days a week, and usually when I was not working on a Saturday or Sunday, I would still be working. I'd go to national and regional conferences with other vendors in the industry, and set up a booth to network, advertise my trade.

A lot of business actually came from those conferences. I'd make contacts or find out about leads on projects, which led to my very first project for the University of Richmond.

It was a small job, creating the new catering kitchen for the alumni center. I think the fee was around $1,200, but it was a huge project for me. It introduced me to architects, which I learned were integral to getting more business in the college dining industry. Architects were responsible for the design of the building, and if they liked you as a consultant, then they'd bring you in to help them with future food service related in the buildings they were designing.

The second big project that I landed was with Bryn Mawr College. This was the first occasion where I employed my in-depth analysis of the campus culture. I interviewed students who used the facilities and discovered that they had a unique situation. The cafeteria was filled with young women who would sit at different tables and speak different languages. It was encouraged on campus. At one table, people would be speaking German, French at another—a wide variety.

So it was very interesting to learn about what they wanted to accomplish, socially.

I did a survey to capture more information about what was unique about the campus, and then I made some rather out-of-the-box recommendations about how to utilize their very limited and challenging space. I recommended things they had never before considered, but I was able to show how it would work in the report I submitted, which was about three-quarters of an inch thick with charts and graphs.

The administrators I submitted it to were blown away by my ideas on how to use the facility. And from that time forward, I started getting calls from architects who were redesigning halls. When I got on the phone with them, they'd tell me that Bryn Mawr said if they were selected, they would be using me as a designer.

One of the most rewarding aspects of my career is being able to return to the universities I've worked with and witness how much their campus has evolved because of our recommendations. In many ways, this success is even better than any monetary reward I might receive.

The University of New Hampshire, for instance, was one of the more challenging projects. We developed a campus-wide dining master plan that included actionable and detailed recommendations on how to evolve their dining program and meal plans in ways that had never before been considered. The director of dining at the time was not too shy to publicly say, after reading our report, that "There is no frickin' way we are going to make these changes."

He slept on it and changed his mind.

This was eight years ago, and back then they had around 4,000 students signed up on their meal plan. Now they have over 9,800 meal plan holders, and one of the most successful self-operated dining programs in North America.

I experienced the same success with Ferris State University. To watch an interview with the President of Ferris State University please go to my website, www.porterkhouwconsulting.com, and click the button on the right hand side of the home page, "Press Play to Watch," for the Ferris State University video of the new Rock Café we programmed and designed. In his review of our work, the President said, "This is one of the most significant and best things that's ever happened to our campus. It's brought the students together in ways we never dreamt."

It's true—they have exponentially grown their business. And I remember at the beginning of it all, when I was telling this client what my plan would achieve, I said, "You're going to expand your hours, increase participation, sell more meal plans, the food cost is going to go down, sales will grow, and labor cost will stay the same."

In the interviews the Director of Dining confirms it. "Yes, David," she says, "that's exactly what happened."

This is a trend that continues to grow. My company recently devised a revolutionary dining program for a university building a new student hub. My recommendations included building a main staircase that would connect several floors. On one floor, they would have opportunities and public and private spaces for individual and group study, free printing, flat screen TVs, foosball tables, and pool tables. And on the top floor, there would be a dining hall where students could come 24/7 to have a meal or snack.

Essentially, they will create the perfect social architecture for their students. They will have a place where they can do it all—work, eat, and socialize. This is a contracted account, and this entire program will be stipulated in the RFP and subsequent contract, right down to the contractor being responsible for all food and social space, and even toner cartridges, paper, and printing supplies. It's all part of the package, as well as part of the value of the program.

The system I've developed is not just about perfecting your dining program—it's about perfecting your social architecture. In my opinion, dining and socializing are inseparable. You can have dining with little or no social consideration, but you will never come close to achieving your optimum social architecture without a properly organized dining program.

I created, and use, the phrase "social architecture" quite often, and it is only because that's what makes our clients and our company successful. We not only create what's best for your campus in terms of business, but in terms of your social architecture as well. And when it comes right down to it, I believe there is no more powerful force—call it "social force"—that will attract and draw students together. As Yoda would say, "May the (social) force be with you."

Follow me to the next chapter, and I'll lay down the blueprint to determining your university's perfect plan.

CHAPTER FOUR

Drafting the Blueprint

DINING IS THE NEXUS of your campus social archi-tecture. It's a fine-spun blanket that can make or break several non-food factors: it can significantly con-tribute to a really great first impression when students and parents come for a campus visit; it can increase retention rates; and it makes for stronger alumni in the long run because of the lifelong friendships made over meals, and the emotional ties forged for your col-lege or university brand.

But that's only if you have the optimum dining program. Not only do you need an optimum program, but you must be able to deliver that program as well. Or find a food service management company that can deliver that program.

As you've learned, that's where my skills converge. After forty-plus years in this business, I will not only implement my unique process to create your optimum dining program with a step-by-step action plan, but I will make a compelling case for it, using market research, experience, and empirical data, too. I will work closely with your dining department or, at your direction, facilitate a selection process that will ensure that your program finds the best operator to take your optimum program and put the plan into action.

This selection process is crucial because most administrators believe that operators will put the unique needs of their campus first and implement a program to meet those needs. This is what I call "fool's gold." It's what keeps me in business: colleges and universities find themselves trapped with these food service management companies who never proactively rise to the challenge of "getting it right" for their campus.

More often than not, the trouble begins when these colleges and universities use their food service contractor as their consultant. Why is that trouble? Because there's a tremendous conflict of interest! Contractors have a fiduciary responsibility to their stockholders, not to what's right for the school. I'll get more into this later, but for now remember: use them to manage your program and to source off-balance-sheet capital, but not as your consultant.

Before you even think about hiring a food service operator, you've got to determine your optimum program and independently appraise its value. But how do you determine what your program should be? Or more importantly, how does my team of skilled and visionary consultants determine what your program should be?

I've glossed over it in previous chapters, but now let's get down to details. Allow me to walk you through our process of perfecting the social architecture of your campus through dining.

The process begins with me and a few of my team members completely immersing ourselves in the unique culture of your campus and community. Our first step is conducting interviews with all of the stakeholders who are directly, or indirectly, related to the food services on campus. This could include the President, Director of Admissions, Dean of Students, CFO, Residential Life staff, Director of Housing, Student Government President—the list goes on.

We ask these decision makers, "What is your vision for the social architecture of your campus?" And then we hit the pavement.

We walk through campus. We follow students. We interview students. We observe. Our goal is to determine what is unique about the campus in terms of its culture, philosophy, and geography. We want to learn what it is that defines your campus.

When I step onto a campus, I put myself in the

students' shoes and then walk, and walk, and walk. While other consultants or vendors look at food services from a financial or logistical perspective, I view it holistically. I sit down with groups of students and ask them questions to determine what dining services are needed on your campus.

One thing that may surprise you is that I don't ask the students, "What do you want?" Rather, I ask, "What do you do?" I ask for complete details on students' dining habits. I want to know a typical day in the life of the student. Where do they go for breakfast? Where do they get snacks? What do they do when it's eleven o'clock at night and their stomachs start growling?

It may seem like a circular method of interviewing, but I've learned through extensive experience that what we do is a better indication of what we will do in the future than what we say we will do.

For example, students may say that they want more organic options, a vegan-friendly menu, or a healthier food message, but in the end, they're going to the local mom and pop pizza place when they're hungry at night. I want to know why they go there, who they call, and when they call. I want to establish their patterns.

I'm not a believer in "If you build it, they will come." Nor am I believer in creating something when there is no demand. Because when it comes down to it, we cannot create the demand.

That is why I am diligent in immersing myself in student life. I want to find out what, when, and where the demand is. If there's a demand, then students are going to find a way to meet it, whether it's on or off campus, at the local dive café, or at a trendy chain restaurant.

I am so passionate about this information that I sometimes find myself wandering around a college campus and the local town at midnight just to know what the students are up to.

One time, I was following a bus filled with students at eleven p.m. to see what route they would take to their residence after getting off of the bus. Did they take the sidewalk and use what the architect intended as the main entrance (and most administrators said they used), or did they cut through the woods, walk past the dumpster, and through the back door by the receiving dock?

If you guessed the latter, take three steps forward. Students tend to take the path of least resistance. So in this case, you have three choices: move the bus stop, lock the back door and force them around front, or honor their pattern and site the food location inside the building despite knowing what they really do.

This type of information would play a big role in determining where the location of the new dining facility should be located. And I was so focused on gathering this information that I was shocked when I saw flashing blue and red lights in my rearview mirror.

Campus security pulled me over because they wanted to know what I was doing following around a bus at eleven o'clock at night. I had some serious explaining to do! But once I told them my story, I can't say they understood what I was doing, but they allowed me to go on about my business.

The reason I put myself through this is to determine the patterns. What are students doing now? How can food services align with these patterns? For instance, if a university wanted to put in another retail spot, then my goal would be to find out where the students go. Where is the parking lot located? If the parking lot is easier to reach than the dining hall, then chances are, students will opt for the drive-thru or wait to eat at their final destination.

But sometimes the success—or failure—of a program has less to do with logistical matters, and more to do with the ultimate value offered.

What do I mean by "value"? I believe we know something is of value by a feeling in the pit of our stomachs, rather than the cortex of our brains. Whether you pay $2,000 or $600 for a laptop, both of which will functionally get the job done, boils down to an emotion. Does this "feel" like a good value? In twenty-three years of conducting focus groups, I have yet to encounter students that go to Starbucks, Whole Foods, or purchase Apple Computer products to save money. Budgets and individual financial resources do matter; however, when a student goes to Mom and Dad and tells them to switch to a lower meal plan or stay on a more expensive meal plan, it doesn't have to do with what it costs, but rather what works for the student day in and day out based on their, the student's, clock.

So in the end, the price doesn't really matter—it's the value of the program that really matters.

I witness a lot of administrators, consultants, and food service management companies wrapping themselves around a pole trying to come up with new meal plans, usually at a lower price with fewer meals. In my opinion, this is an attempt to make an undesirable dining program more desirable by charging less for it.

In reality, the student's desire to get off a meal plan has little to nothing to do with the price of the meal plan, even though that becomes the student's battle cry to get off the plan. The meal plan is nothing more and nothing less than a method of payment. The more important question is what are they getting from the food service program in exchange for what their meal plan permits them to purchase.

In a nutshell, what I do is identify what the issues really are and then answer these and many more questions that arise during our engagements.

Why do students reject a meal plan? We know students are on a different clock and they want to eat at ten or eleven, but what happens when the dining hall closes at seven? They can't use their meal plans. So the meal plan is of no use to them.

To put it simply, the students reject the plan because it has no value.

Our answer is to create more value. The ability to socialize and see and be seen is part of this value proposition along with the food, hours, etc. When we line up all of these planets and it all comes together, your students are going to tell Mom and Dad, "Enroll me in the meal plan another year." It hits all the right notes because the value has fundamentally changed. And we find that value through our interviews and research.

We collect a lot of empirical data to corroborate what we find during our time spent on campus. Everything from financials to enrollment, housing, and occupancy—we want to know it all. What are the projections for the next three to five years? Are there any strategic plans in place to grow the campus? This is especially critical if the university plans to grow geographically. We want to make sure dining locations will remain in the center, where they will be most easily accessed.

After we conduct the on-campus research and speak

to staff, faculty, and students, we look for quantitative data to support our findings. That's where our online survey comes in. We send out a comprehensive survey to everyone affected by food services and ask—at last—for participants to tell us what they want.

The results from this survey support the evidence that we've already gathered through qualitative research methods. But now instead of saying, "Put in a sushi bar because we spoke with thirty students in a focus group and they suggested it," we can show you that, in fact, three thousand students would utilize a sushi option on your campus.

Finally, after we gather the information, my team has a caucus. We brainstorm, discuss our findings, come up with pros and cons, and formulate our recommendations. And then we take this information and have an interactive work session with our client. This multi-tiered approach is not only thorough—it goes beyond what any other consultant would offer.

This may sound like a bit of a stretch, but I picture myself as a detective. I sleuth around campus, go incognito, conduct rounds of questioning, and then present my findings before the jury (our client). The whole process takes about three to four weeks—that includes the time it takes to get a feel for the campus, conduct interviews and surveys, and compare the results.

We call this last step our "interactive work session" because it's just that—interactive. We want to hear any ideas that the client might like to contribute to what we've already found. We encourage clients to push back, challenge us, and give us feedback so that we have a better understanding of what they do, or do not, like.

The major sticking point for most people when faced with a major business decision is the financials. A package can have all the bells and whistles, but it ultimately comes down to the money. This is also something that my team anticipates.

Using the data we've gathered, we will do financial projections for the university based upon our business plan. That includes both revenue and expense projections. We can show through hard data how sales can dramatically increase over the next ten years through our plan. And the beauty of it all is that it doesn't cost the students a penny more.

For example, I was working with a university that was going to be the first college in the area that operates twenty-four hours a day, seven days a week. It was the optimum plan for the school, but I had to make a case to convince them to go against "the norm" (as defined by their operator). So I put the numbers side by side and showed them how, over the next ten years, if they went with the plan they would increase revenue by $37 million and grow their surplus (profit) proportionally without increasing the price of the meal plan to the students.

"But David, that's impossible," the President said in reply (I get that a lot).

And then I showed him the financial data that we collected and turned into a presentation. We covered everything from the cost of the meal plan to the cost of food and labor, went line by line through each of the operating expenses and showed them exactly how it would work. And in the end, they were awestruck.

"You were absolutely right, David!" they said (I get that a lot, too).

In the same way you'd make a case before a judge and jury, we present our findings to the board of decision makers and, in turn, they start to open themselves up to a new way of thinking.

The proof is in the pudding. And that's our job—to figure out how to guide our clients from point A to point B and show that it's possible. In many cases, these are radical changes. Not radical in the sense that they're crazy, but radical because the food service operator has never suggested program recommendations similar to mine, and the school has never considered my recommendations before, even though empirically, it makes perfect sense.

The icing on the cake is when the bids come in. No

matter how radical a twenty-four-hour venue or free printing service may seem, all doubts are put to rest when the contractors respond.

Sometimes, the operators are similarly shocked when they see our requests. But I can tell you that if the school stands behind what they need with the support of the independent research and advice that produced the new program, then the operators will find a way to meet, and in some cases exceed, their requests.

For instance, I recently met with the contractors who serviced the university that requested an upgrade to twenty-four-hour service. Right out of the chute they said there's no other university in Canada that has a twenty-four-hour residential dining hall with continuous service. "It's a nice idea, but we are not going to do that here," they replied.

I politely reminded them that the new program recommendations have been uniquely suited to meet the needs of that particular campus, not all of the others. This bold program was what their school needed. The school came to them first because of their history together. And even though we advised that they open it up to all bidders, we respect our client's wishes. These contractors were welcome to respond with their own plan, but if they didn't, they would do so at the peril of the school going with one of the other competitive bidders.

They had the option to either put up or shut up. And they put up. They met every one of the client's requests! When the bids came in, the school was shocked and conflicted. "You were right, David. But why didn't they suggest this kind of program before?" they asked. "We have heard nothing like this from them over the past ten years of their tenure here at our school."

They didn't have the vision that we had, nor did they have someone to see it to fruition.

Sometimes when we go to conferences, we'll see people we've worked with and they'll say "David, when you made those recommendations, they pointed us in a direction that none of us had considered. It wasn't even on our radar. But you know what, you were right."

This is music to my ears. It makes me feel as though I have brought real and meaningful value to the students, faculty, and staff of that campus. It has nothing to do with my ego; rather, it has everything to do with the fact that the process worked.

We are agents of change, in every sense of the term. Even though this change translates to an overwhelming success for the dining program and social fabric of the campus, as an agent of change, I sometimes push people out of their comfort zone. We come on strong and in the end have a very low profile as the new plans are successfully implemented.

As Ronald Reagan once said, "There is no limit to what you can accomplish if you don't care who gets the credit." This is one of my guiding principles with the work I do.

What we learned as we immersed ourselves brought us to that conclusion. The interviews, focus groups, collecting empirical data, becoming one with the community on campus, and identifying the challenges and issues led us to that solution. There's nothing more rewarding than when we figure it out for our clients.

I think of it this way: When you construct a new building, the first thing you do is put up the steel framing. That framing is what holds up the rest of the façade—the marble tiles, the stucco doorways, the shiny trimmings, and all.

The dining program is the steel structure for the social architecture of your campus. I am your social architect.

We collect the data and create the blueprint. We put up the steel framing, and find the best operator to complete the trimmings. We will change the social architecture of your campus in order to create a better and brighter future for your colleagues, staff, and students.

CHAPTER FIVE

Packaging Your Program

AFTER ALL, YOU WOULDN'T go to a heart surgeon for a knee replacement. And you'd scoff at the notion of doing it yourself. You would want the person who's performed hundreds of successful knee replacement operations with happy patients who enjoyed long and active lives thereafter.

This applies to numerous other fields as well, and believe it or not, dining services is one of them.

There are so many factors that go into creating, negotiating, and executing your dining services program. And there are even more pitfalls that threaten to make your program anything but the best. In a perfect world, everyone would get a fair shake in any given business dealing. But we know that this is far from the case.

Several years ago, I was before a group of fifty Auxiliary Services Directors presenting a successful food service operator selection process that I had recently completed for a university in New York. I asked for a show of hands of how many attendees had a contracted food service. All but two raised their hand. Then I asked of those who raised their hand, how many had a contractor who was crying poor mouth and complaining about losing money? They all raised their hand.

As you know, time and time again, colleges are getting taken advantage of by operators who are more concerned with their fiduciary responsibility to their stockholders rather than what's best for the school.

We want you to be as prepared as possible when entering into the process of putting together a dining program. And because we know the complexity of the process, we'd like to walk you through the steps to creating your optimum dining program, as well as the most important factors to be aware of in these situations.

The first step is to be aware of the pitfalls that many of our clients have encountered. I say this is the first step because those pitfalls are the hardest to see when you're in the early stages of negotiations, and can really set you up for disaster.

Take, for instance, the capital investment. You know, the lump of money offered under the guise of a signing bonus, gift, contribution, investment, etc.? A deal like that would make you look like a hero, securing much-needed funds to revamp your state-of-the–art, 1970s' dining facilities and an operator that will take your dining services to the next level—right? Wrong. It can be difficult to see a multi-million-dollar offering as a pitfall, but indeed it is just that, unless carefully negotiated by an expert representing your interests.

The awful truth is that these capital investments are nothing more than a high interest loan from the Bank of _____ (fill in your contractor here), and unless all of the complexities of the contract are addressed, negotiated, and memorialized properly, this high-interest loan from your contractor could turn into a hostage fee. As I mentioned earlier in the book, this money only comes under the certain terms that the company will receive it back.

Another name for these cancellation terms is "buyout language." I cringe every time I say it, but this buyout language would make the gangsters from *Goodfellas* jealous. Here, you receive a $5 million investment amortized over ten years. You have been seduced into a false sense of security, because among other things, you have skillfully negotiated a termination clause, usually with 180 days' notice. You're emboldened because you know you can play the termination card and get rid of them if they don't deliver on their promises. But you don't need to worry about that because they've assured you they have the star management

players and the deepest bench of top management for
your campus. What could ever go wrong?

It's all good—pop the champagne and let the cel-
ebrations begin! But now, let's say, you're five years
into this ten-year contract and you're frustrated with
the low caliber of the general manager, customer service, lack of responsiveness (you fill in the blank), and
you have threatened to pull the pin and terminate the
contract a number of times over the past two years.
You've reached your last straw and you're prepared to
cancel. But then either you, your purchasing department, or your general counsel reviews the contract
and notices the clause regarding "buyout language."

Translation: If the operator turns out to be less
than ideal, or even downright terrible? Too bad, so
sad. You'll have to either write a large check for the
unamortized portion of the investment (high interest
loan), in this case two and one half million dollars, or
suffer through a few more years of subpar service to
avoid having to write the check.

That leads me to the next pitfall: know your program's worth.

I see it again and again: schools are not getting
anywhere near the financial benefit that is due them.
It's similar to if someone found a Monet oil painting in
their attic, but had no idea who this "Monet character"

was, so they take it to an art dealer who takes advantage of their ignorance and pays them five bucks for it. It seems like an extreme comparison, but unfortunately, it's accurate.

My gift is to see the dining opportunities on your campus that no one else sees. I will evaluate your dining program, and not only develop a vision and action plan for the optimum program for your campus, but also independently appraise the value of your program so that when you go into a negotiation with a contractor, you will know exactly what it is worth, what your projected revenues, expenses, and profit or commissions should be. In addition, I will calculate how much upfront capital is realistic and how to structure the terms of that investment so that you mitigate your risk and exposure while ensuring the contractor is responsive and does their job.

But even if a school knows its value and knows to avoid the capital investment trap, some universities aren't able to express their value in the contract. Again, I am probably dating myself, but do you remember a commercial for financial services with a successful man walking toward you after just exiting a big, executive helicopter and saying, "It's not how much money you make, it's how much of it you keep"? Well, the same holds true for these high-stakes contract negotiations.

The contractors have what I consider to be the most advanced and sophisticated sales and contract negotiation teams.

A lot of the contracts my team reviews tend to be very nebulous with little to no financial or programmatic detail. So once the contract is signed, if any issues arise—and no doubt, they will arise—there is no legal obligation on the part of the operator to address them.

With a lack of specificity in the contract, the operator usually ends up invoicing the school for expense items that were never discussed. This is extremely frustrating for the school, but right or wrong, they must pay because if they don't, then they compromise their dining program even more.

To recap, if you want to stand a chance negotiating with these mega-corporations, you must: a) be wary of capital investments; b) know the value of your program and what you need; and c) zero in on those needs in extreme detail in the actual contract.

And this is where the issue gets infinitely more complex, but never fear—we're going to walk you through that, too.

As you know, our first step in rebidding a food services contract is to spend time on campus and determine what your school needs in order to have the highest levels of participation by students, faculty, and staff in your dining program that will result in the maximum positive impact on the social architecture and student engagement at your school. We conduct extensive qualitative and quantitative research utilizing both people and numerical data to develop a program that is extraordinary, financially viable, and bankable without raising the cost of meal plans to your students and keeping retail and catering competitive and affordable.

Once you review, challenge, revise, and approve our recommendations to you and your school, we develop a Request for Proposal (RFP) with no ambiguity. We spell out—in exhaustive detail—exactly what your program is going to be.

Completely contrary to the conventional approach, we do not ask what the contractor believes the program should be for your campus. Rather, we stipulate what the program will be. In response to the RFP, bidders must explain how their company, with their resources, expertise, and management teams, will successfully operate this program on a daily basis throughout the term of the agreement.

One of the first questions or objections that is typically raised by one of our clients is: "David, we want the RFP to be ambiguous because we do not want in any way to stifle the creativity of the operator when they respond."

My response is to suggest they go to any of their

colleagues who have had contractors on their campus for any length of time and ask them how that strategy worked out.

Extreme detail goes into the RFP because we want to make sure it will secure precisely the program that we crafted for your school. Our goal is for this to be a win-win for the school and the contractor. Therefore, we provide as much information and transparency as possible so that there are no surprises once the new contract commences.

We are crystal clear about the responsibilities of the university and the responsibilities of the contractor, right down to a table of authorized and unauthorized expenses the contractor will be permitted to expense against this account. This covers everything from utilities to office furniture and equipment. We typically itemize between thirty to fifty cost centers and describe who provides the service.

A few hot-button expenses that the operator usually tries to pass off to the school are trash removal, janitorial services, pest control, and repair and maintenance of all food service equipment. When we accept bids from operators, we require that they include those calculations as part of their financial proposal. We prepare a financial template that the bidders fill out with every revenue, expense, and labor calculation for each business unit in each business segment for each year, including optional years of the proposed term of your agreement. That way, we won't find ourselves sitting around the contract table later on and having to negotiate through all of these points, which can be very arduous and most likely impossible unless the information is collected in the manner and detail we prescribe in our RFPs.

The key is to state everything up front. If you have all of the details in the beginning, then there's never any question of who pays for what.

After we have the financial details, we spell out the program details. This includes items such as venues, menu profiles, meal periods, and hours of operation. What kind of payment methods will be accepted? What will be the key staffing positions? Will they need a manager, executive director, or a residential manager?

Some of these points might seem like obvious operator responsibilities, but we've learned through experience that if it's not in the contract, it's not on the operator. Let's say you do not effectively define and negotiate your catering at the time your contract is signed. Even if your account is big enough, it does not guarantee the operator will automatically provide a catering manager to oversee catering unless they are compelled to do so by the programatic requirements set forth in the RFP. Again, we take care of that so the school does not get mistreated. Again, we take care of that so the school does not get mistreated.

Once we've completed the RFP, we then go through an extensive evaluation period when the bids come in. My team has a scoring criteria based on the specific needs of a particular campus. This not only ensures that the bidders' responses meet the school's demands, but it also provides objectivity in evaluating a number of bids.

My team has actually developed a financial template that is tailored to each one of our clients. When we issue the RFP, we submit the template for the operators to fill out as well. This template details the optimum program that we determined and asks the bidder for information such as sales projections by day with an average door rate for residential venues. That feeds into an annual total sales revenue for each one of the venues, as well as other important information.

In addition, we have bidders complete staffing matrices for each year per business unit by hour, projected throughout the years of the contract. That enables us to go through this information and determine if their sales projections are accurate—albeit realistic—or if they're cutting any corners.

This also allows us to see if their program is in line with the program that we stipulated. For instance, if they haven't correctly, or thoroughly, filled out the

staffing models in compliance with the hours we stipulated, we'd be able to determine that. We'd also be able
to tell if the hourly wages, benefit packages, and other
criteria are consistent with other bidders.

We've encountered bid responses where they've
blatantly ignored our requests, but we wouldn't know
it unless we had these templates. I can't tell you how
many times we've gone through a response and looked
at the staffing model only to find that a location we
requested to be open until midnight was only staffed
until eight p.m. So even though they said one thing,
we can check to make sure what they presented was
accurate and not just fluff.

If you're going out to bid, then I highly recommend
you create a similar financial template that captures
all of this information. It can be tricky to create your
own if you've never done this before, so we've provided
an example that you can download at my website:
http://www.porterkhouwconsulting.com/operator-services/index.html

Defining the program, and then having the bidder put together a portfolio with staffing matrices and
financial information, ensures the integrity of their
response. Additionally, it ensures your ability to objec-
tively evaluate multiple responses.

Once you do select an operator, it's natural to
think that you can finally take a deep sigh of relief. In
fact, this is one of the most challenging phases of the

project—trying to get the bidder to agree in writing to execute what was settled in the bid. If you don't have experience in this type of negotiation, you could soon find yourself equipped with nothing more than a knife at a gunfight.

Perhaps now that we've illustrated the complexity of the negotiation, you can understand why my team has had the privilege to work with so many colleges and universities across the nation. It can be one of the most lucrative deals you could negotiate for your campus, but only if you know what you don't know, and know how to change that.

Now that you have your bachelor's in negotiating with the big leagues, let's take the next step and get your master's. In the next chapter, you're going to learn all about the top food operators on the market. By the finish, not only will you know their game, but you'll be able to spot their signature moves from a mile away.

CHAPTER SIX

The Real Value

NOW THAT YOU'RE educated on the intricacies of food dining programs, you have a fighting chance against the incumbent operators who just aren't cutting it. You know their game, you know what you need, and—most importantly—you know when to say "no."

A lot of times, our clients have found that even after they've read this book, they still want us to put together their dining program because of our knowledge and expertise. We not only know what to look for, but we also know how to negotiate with these companies, and we've done so time and time again. We know the tricks that can only be learned through experience.

One of the first questions our clients have is about our fee, which makes sense—after all, they've been taken advantage of for so long by their food vendor, it's no wonder they'd be wary of any further costs. But the fact of the matter is, we are only successful when you are successful. We're only paid once you've secured your financial and programmatic goals that we've laid out in the RFP.

Now that we're nearing the end of our crash course on dining programs, allow me to give a quick recap on what we do. As you know, there are two phases to our work. First, we independently look at all of the issues and opportunities on your campus that would most greatly benefit the social architecture of your school. Then we make a set of recommendations to you that could affect anything from new locations, concepts, methods of services, meal plans, hours of operation, operating days per year, catering, facilities, and finance. And now the ball is in your court.

You and your committee review our recommendations and tell us what you like, what you don't like, and any and all changes you would like to see. And based upon your feedback, you decide what will go into the RFP. I don't have final say over the dining program. You do.

Phase two consists of RFP development and operator selection process. I take that information and, with a great level of detail, my team puts that into the RFP, and that's what we use to bid the agreement. We don't ask the bidders what they think the program should be. We tell them what it's going to be. As opposed to the conventional approach, where the school provides either no program, or the framework of a program, and asks the bidders to fill in all the blanks, we're going to now tell the operator what they will be providing. Most importantly, we will lay out your program, which is directly linked to your financial goals, that should be met by the operator.

It is not a take it or leave it proposition for bidders. We encourage bidders to elaborate or build on the program we stipulate on your behalf. We in no way want to stifle their creativity. We even encourage them to propose an alternate dining solution if for some reason they believe we have missed the mark. And we frame the financial objectives as goals. We make it clear that it is at their discretion as to whether the bid is lower than, meets, or exceeds the financial goals including a required minimum annual dollar guarantee for their bid submission.

Not only do we negotiate to get your campus what it needs in terms of quality, but the fully executed contract that is produced by this process will include financial guarantees for every year of the contract. We do this by securing an annual minimum dollar amount from the operator in the form of a bottom-line number or annual percentage—whichever is greater.

What that means is that if the contractor falls back into the same old rut where they're doing a mediocre job and the sales go down, or they're cutting corners and students don't want to participate in the meal plan anymore, then the contract requires that the operator still pay the school a guaranteed minimum, annually. The reason for this is twofold: it provides financial security for the school, and a financial incentive for the operator to do their job.

Operators respond to financial pain. Unfortunately, as many of my clients have learned the hard way before coming to me, they don't respond to your financial pain, but rather their own. If they're put in a position where they're required to pay a guaranteed annual minimum, then you can bet your bottom dollar that they will get it right and maintain the projected level of performance.

We create an environment that incentivizes the operators to perform. A lot of contracts—the conventional contracts—create a hostage situation where the school is held hostage to the operator because of onerous financial terms that the school has agreed to. The operator doesn't have the incentive to put the right management team in place, because they know that if they're in a big capital investment, the school isn't likely to write them a check for a huge amount of money to get rid of them.

Our process produces an extraordinarily detailed and complete contract that guarantees the performance and financial goals. It's written in a document that is contractually sound and sealed, and fully executed at the conclusion of our work. And as I said before, we only win when your students, faculty, and staff win. So when the contract is signed with all the i's dotted and t's crossed, that's when we collect our fee, which is capped at ten percent of the difference from what you were previously receiving in the form of financial remuneration and what the new contract provides you in the form of financial remuneration.

I do not want my company to be rewarded for getting you what you already have. I only want to be compensated if we improve your financial position. It is my heartfelt belief that by getting it right, first and foremost, for your students, we are able to create a business model and financial construct that will benefit your school. I call this a success fee.

We don't see a penny until after all of our work is done and we've made good on our promises. As an example, let's say that right now you're earning $1.2 million per year from your contract. This could be commissions to your school or an override. Let's say we project an increase to $1.5 million in commissions per year. But what if the contractor ends up agreeing to pay you only $1.2 million per year in commissions? That means that you don't pay us anything. Zilch! That may seem insane, but consider it a testament to my confidence in my team's ability to develop a program that increases student participation and gets you that deal.

Once we secure that contract paying you in commissions $1.5 million—and let's say it's a five-year contract, which means an extra $300,000 in commissions to you per year—then our success fee would be ten percent of that $1.5 million in new commissions over the five-year term of the contract, or $150,000 for our services.

This includes any and all costs incurred during our research: airfare to fly to your campus, hotel and car rental costs, etc. None of that is billed to you; rather, that comes out of our success fee. But not even our success fee comes out of your pocket!

When we receive competitive bids from potential operators, they come with a guarantee, which, if that company prevails, is an advance payment of commissions to your school. For example, if three bidders bid on a piece of business, we would receive three cashiers checks in the neighborhood of $400,000 each. We deposit each into an account created solely for the purpose of holding these bid guarantees in escrow. Once the school selects the final company and negotiations are complete, the two companies that did not prevail are returned their checks. The one company that does prevail has their check processed. And if our success fee was based off of that $1.5 million, then we would invoice $150,000 from that guarantee, and forward the balance, $250,000, to the school.

We get paid once, and that's only when the new program commences or the contract is executed.

Why are we worth it? What are high retention and recruitment capture rates worth? What is a world-class dining program worth? What are your students worth? We will go where no man/woman has gone before. Our number one focus is not financial—it's about getting you a better program. And we never settle for anything less. I'll refer to my experience on the Canadian campus as an example. I put together a package that they thought was too good to be true and made them reluctant to go forward in the bidding process.

Even the incumbent operator said, "Nobody in Canada does that. We're not going to do that." But when I told him, in the presence of my clients, with all due respect, sir, you don't get to make that decision, and that the school had engaged our firm to see this through the contract renegotiation process and if necessary the competitive bidding process, he changed his tune. Not only did they sign the contract that we composed and negotiated, but they also commented on how wonderful the idea was, how profound the approach was, how it was the best solution a college could come up with, and why they had all of the qualifications to execute it.

While this is a big win for the school, it's also outrageous. This company had serviced them for the previous ten years. Once the school realized that the operator had the power to give them what they needed all along, they wanted to know why they didn't whistle that tune before. To say there were a few bitter administrators who had consumed ten years of contractor Kool-Aid that essentially got them to the highest negatives ever experienced by the school from the students regarding the dining program would be an understatement. My response to that was, it's totally predicable how you feel; unfortunately, it is the way the game is played, and now it is a new day with a new program and a new contract, and we must move forward.

The fact of the matter is, I don't know anyone else who will put their neck on the line like I do. Not once, but again and again. I am so passionate, and believe in my purpose so much, that I've even bet my own professional fee so that a client would move forward with the program that would be best for their campus. This applies to any school I work with. If we ever fall short of what we dictate in the contract—or if we create a contract that has no bidders—then we will rebid the program for free. Bottom line.

I won't say that there aren't others who will do it for less. You've probably encountered consultants who offer their services for maybe a fraction of our fee. And quite frankly, you could probably even get one of those to get you a contract that's technically sound and fully executed. But what do you end up with? You end up with a great contract memorializing the same old song and dance. And your students are still clamoring to get off their meal plans and there goes those millions, left on the table.

So what's the real cost?

Do you want a gunslinger who will go up against anybody to protect your interests and take them to the mat to make sure you get a fair arrangement? Or do you want somebody who will get bullied, regardless of their title, because some big deal company says, "Nobody does it like that, so we're not going to do it like that." And in the end, you give away the value of your program.

Even if you have a good program, if it isn't negotiated properly then you'll never get it. On the other hand, you can get somebody to negotiate a great contract for you, but if you don't have a great program that will better serve the students, then all you're going to do is maintain the status quo with a good contract, but no added value. You can't have one without the other.

If that's okay with you, then you shouldn't pay more than $20k for it. As a matter of fact, you probably don't even need somebody to rebid it for you. Simply extend the contract you have right now.

It's my team's vision and experience combined with a successfully negotiated agreement that seals the deal—and that's something that money simply can't buy.

In what other business can you find someone who will not only get you a better program, without raising the price of mandatory meal plans, and more money to boot, and do it at no cost out of your pocket?

At the end of the day, those clients who may have begrudged us our fees initially are more than happy to grant us our ten percent because the deals they secured have been so beneficial and lucrative.

These same clients have compared us to Cirque de Soleil, because what Cirque de Soleil did for the circus, we're doing for dining services and your social architecture: we're changing the game. And while the price of admission might be a bit more, the magic that happens once the curtain lights go up is well worth it.

CHAPTER SEVEN

Beware of Strangers Bearing Gifts

I'M GOING TO COME right out and say it: If you're reading this book, you are special. You're the one who cares enough about your school's success to educate yourself on one of the most important contributing factors. Maybe you're even the one responsible for making the big decisions for your school, and have done so again and again.

But this is decision-making to the nth degree. Dining services is a different animal, unlike any other negotiation, and it attracts a different kind of predator—multibillion dollar, multinational conglomerates called food service management companies. Are they friend, foe, or Trojan horse? If you prescribe to the notion of "buyer beware" and come to the table with an advocate who will zealously represent and protect you, then you need not worry.

The key to out-foxing your predator is to know as much about "the game" as they do. And if you work with me, you will know more.

When it comes time to rebid your dining services contract, you may come in contact with any or all of the three big corporations: Chartwells, Sodexo, and Aramark. There are roughly nine other companies that top the list of frequently used vendors, but to tell you the truth, they're all pretty much the same. I am often asked, "Who is the best?" "Who's my favorite?" And to that I answer, "There is no 'best' or 'favorite.'" In just about every instance, I could recall accounts held by each company that would blow your mind in a positive way, as well as accounts held by the same companies that would turn your stomach.

Each corporation is broken up into regional territories like the Northeast, Mid-Atlantic, Southeast, and Midwest. Each region has its own Vice President, District Managers, General Managers, and culinary and marketing resources.

But again, their tactics really don't vary much from team to team. When it comes down to it, the question of who can do a better job depends on who can communicate their ability to execute the program and manage it on a day-to-day basis with all of the resources they have to offer in response to our RFP.

These representatives are very sophisticated sales

teams and will do whatever it takes to win your contract. And why shouldn't they? That's what they get paid to do, and that's what their fiduciary responsibility to their stockholders entails. But just how lucrative—or self-serving—that contract is depends on how much you know about the value of your program and the negotiation, combined with how much you know about your adversary. Regardless of how accomplished you are, how successful you've been, your peak physical condition and knowledge, would you climb Mount Everest without a Sherpa?

These behemoth corporations send out their best. Their representatives are sophisticated and highly trained sales people with a lot of experience, and they'll be able to size you up in no time. They will know within a very short period of time whether you are someone who not only knows what your program is worth and knows how to negotiate, but knows the value of your program, or if you're a first-time customer. And that's when you become a sitting duck. And it won't matter what you've done, what you know, or who you are, it's a universal truth—if you represent yourself, then you have a fool for a client.

These sales reps are used to dealing with sitting ducks. They're used to being able to not only tell universities what their program should be and how much it's worth, but they're also used to winning them over.

These people will wine you, dine you, take you out to golf, present you with fancy swag at the meetings, and then they'll tell you all of the improvements that you need to make, and in some cases offer hundreds of thousands or millions of dollars up front to win you over.

They'll say that it's difficult for them to see the business opportunity in a program that needs so many improvements. The dining halls need renovation, the menu needs to be updated—and it's all going to cost a lot of cashola.

Not to mention, most of these operators have prime vendor agreements and when you sign your agreement, you are essentially committing your school to a prime vendor agreement with the operator. That means that their vendors have agreed to pay them rebates on all food purchased through these contracts. In most cases, you will never see any of that or be in a position to independently audit those rebates. For example, if you have a piece of business that's worth $10 million a year and your food cost is fifty percent, then that means $5 million a year of the campus procurement money is funneled through their contracts.

Add into the equation that any operator may have numerous contracts with vendors, and you can begin to get an idea of how much money they can make off the back end from distributors and manufacturers.

So when these sales reps come to your campus and give you the old song and dance about all of the improvements that need to be made, one of their suggestions will most likely be to add in more channels for their vendors' high cost products, bottled beverages, prepackaged food products, etc.

They'll tell you about how college dining needs to have more portability. Students are on the run and they want to grab and go. And then they'll pitch you their really neat concept for a store with beverages and pre-packaged food to serve these on-the-go students.

In other words, they want you to open up a glorified C Store.

The school will then ask, "Can you really do this for us?"

And right when you begin to think dismal thoughts about how your program really is worthless, that's when they'll hook you to the tune of a multimillion dollar capital investment.

Joe Sales Rep will say, "It might be hard, but let me see what I can do. Your facilities are in real trouble. They're dated. I'm not sure if we can make this work, but I'm going to go back to the home office."

He'll come back within forty-eight hours and say, "You want this to be a five-year contract? If you give me a ten-year or a fifteen-year contract, then we can give you $3 million to renovate those facilities."

This sounds like a dream! But after the bricks and mortar are laid, and the doors open for business, you'll soon find yourself in anything but.

They'll call that cash an investment in your partnership, but this is when you must ask yourself: Why would anyone give millions of dollars to a program they were only minutes before calling worthless?

The answer is that they know the value, and they know that you do not.

It is crucial that you go into the negotiation knowing what you want to achieve and why you're worth it. But in order to know what you want, you need to understand the opportunity in the business model.

If you've learned anything by now, it's that this is a model with a million moving parts. It's downright difficult to learn this transaction in one go, even with this step-by-step guide through the process.

You've heard this story of a negotiation gone awry before—that campus in the Midwest lives to tell the tale. This is the school with a convenience store in place of an actual dining hall to connect their freshman students. And if you remember, their recruitment numbers are far from satisfactory.

How do you think they were sold on this idea? By these big corporations looking for a way to serve their purposes, rather than the school's and the students'.

But if you have someone at the table who is

experienced—someone who has worked with dozens of universities and successfully fought for their optimum program—then you're dealing with a different customer.

When these sales reps see me at the table, they know that I come with a steel spine to serve but one master—YOU!

It just makes practical sense to have someone in your corner. Would you go to court without a lawyer? Would you undergo surgery without the advice of a doctor?

I'm sure the answer to both is a resounding "no," and yet so many universities are going into just as tricky situations without an advocate on their behalf.

These sales people represent billion dollar conglomerates. As friendly as they seem, they're not your next-door neighbors who want to get into the catering business. They've been around the block and have billions of dollars of purchasing power, which is only a testament to all of the battles they've won.

When I first work with a new client, it takes them a while to believe me when I tell them how much their program is worth. And even if they reluctantly go along with me, they rarely believe it until the bidders actually return with their bids.

Suddenly, the game changes.

Before the operator even has a chance to size your

school up, I will tell you exactly how we can add value to your program. This could be in the form of unlimited dining access, beautiful new facilities, more hours of operation, reformed meal plans—whatever it takes to achieve your optimum program.

In addition, I tell you how you can add a couple million dollars per year to the bottom line, if for no other reason than simply changing the food cost structure.

Before, you were prepared to give away millions to a food company in exchange for their "capital investment," all of which would go toward renovations. But with this money, you can use it to renovate the facility and the science lab, the library—whatever you please!

The moral of the story is that these sales reps are strangers bearing gifts.

They present themselves as your new best friend when, in fact, there's a huge conflict of interest. Anyone who is going to recommend how you should structure your dining services, and how they're the best people for it, is really only serving themselves.

Ultimately, they want to get the best deal possible for their company and put all the risk on the university. The risk should be shared, particularly the financial risk.

The smooth tactics and grandiose promises of the sales representative is enough to sway even the most experienced negotiators. After all, who wouldn't want to jump out of their chair at the promise of a multi-million dollar signing bonus, as well as a complete revamping of your outdated facilities?

But the truth is that beneath the veneer there lurks the hungry beast. Now, I don't in any way mean to say that these people are bad. They simply don't have your best interests in mind.

Why is that?

As I mentioned before, they have a responsibility to their stockholders, not to your school. So they'll make whatever decisions are necessary in order to get the most for their company.

In my experience, I haven't found one corporate team that really understands college and university dining services. I think they understand that they want to get the account, but when it comes to things like social architecture, they haven't a clue.

They know how to sell brands, they know how to take advantage of meal plan revenue bases, but they don't know how to develop a dining program that truly fits the unique needs of the campus. And in the end, they're not only setting the campus up for failure, but they're selling themselves short in terms of the school's mutually beneficial success.

So what do you think of those fancy meals and golf trips now?

Point is: Beware strangers bearing gifts.

Treat this negotiation as you would any other multimillion dollar, high-stakes business deal and call in the professionals. Don't try this at home! Get an advocate. Get someone who will fight for you.

CHAPTER EIGHT

Navigating Rough Waters

AT THIS POINT, WE'VE gone through the entire bidding process, from creating your program to securing the agreement. Ultimately, the end game of all this is to make a decision. And once you make a decision, you have to stick with it, so how do you make sure the operator you choose is "the one?"

In this chapter, we'll discuss this all-important stage of the evaluation process so that in the end you can feel confident with your winning candidate.

As we mentioned earlier, we've developed our own system to evaluate candidates. It's based on a special weighting system to ensure all bidders are on a level playing field. But what exactly is that playing field?

When bidders respond to the RFP, they are required to fill out spreadsheets that we have created. We then use that information for our formulas that in turn give us a score.

That's the process in a nutshell, but as the saying goes, the devil is in the details so let's go in-depth and begin with step one.

The first step in the process is what we call a pre-bid conference. This usually occurs within a week of issuing the bid and is held at the university. The purpose of this meeting is to go over important milestones and give the prospective bidders an overview of the process. If there are any unique or specific programmatic or financial goals, we discuss them here.

After the pre-bid conference, we hold a question and answer session, giving bidders the opportunity to ask for clarification on any of the terms we've established. Sometimes the bidders don't feel compelled to ask questions immediately, so we allow for a couple of days after the conference during which time they may submit additional questions. We always provide detailed answers to any questions we may receive.

Once the meeting is complete, we offer a tour of the facilities. This is extremely important because we believe it is impossible for an operator to be able to tell how they would run a university's program without seeing the university.

After the pre-bid conference is over, we start receiving bids within three to four weeks. And that's when we bust out the elbow grease and go into evaluation mode.

As I mentioned, we submit a spreadsheet along with the RFP for bidders to fill out in total detail. The spreadsheet asks for details including menu variety and selection, hours of operation, and staffing expectations. These categories are later scored and weighted depending on what is most important to the school.

In essence, we ask the bidders to submit a business plan. In this plan, they must acknowledge and describe what their approach is going to be to our unique program that is already fully detailed in the RFP.

Their task is to illustrate how they are going to execute, and even add to, the program based upon their service philosophies and experience.

The template, which I described in an earlier chapter, is how we can assure that they've complied with all of our requirements. Through items that they fill out such as staffing matrices, we can determine that their business plan will achieve what the school has independently determined is right for them.

We lock the template so that the companies cannot change the format, and also so that we can ensure that they fill it out completely. This pro forma contains all of the information that the client needs to be able to tell whether the projected food sales costs make sense as a percentage of sales as a dollar amount. It also allows universities to take the business plans and compare them with each other.

That's where our scoring system comes into action.

It's one thing to look at these charts and see projected figures and mission statements, but it's entirely more helpful to give value to these terms so that the school can know, beyond a doubt, that one particular operator has outscored the others.

Although methods of comparison are common among businesses going through this process, my team has developed a unique scoring system to rate all of the bidders in a fair and substantive way.

Having an equal playing field is key to coming up with a solid decision, and having a weighted system that adjusts according to what is most important for the school makes it a thorough and specific evaluation.

We examine a lot of different criteria. We analyze retail operations, and within that information look at program, menus, and concept description. We look at pricing and portions for each one of the venues in retail to make sure it's in line. For instance, one bidder might have four ounces of salmon filets for $9.95, while another offers four ounces for $6.95. This information factors into which operator will give us the best deal.

We examine management organization. We even request that we personally meet with the management candidate and include this in the overall score. When I first started out in the business, this simply wasn't done. But I've noticed that operators are catching on, and some even offer a meeting with their management candidate up front.

We request to meet with the management candidate because they will be the one who is responsible for running the program after the dust clears and the doors open. Their involvement will make or break the success of the program, so we want to be sure that whoever comes with the operator will be the right person for the job.

Along with candidate interviews, we take labor and training practices into consideration, as well as transition planning in order to ensure the new operator's switch-off is smooth and clear-cut.

We also look at financial bids, and this carries the most weight across the board. We look at the financial overview of what the operator projected and how that meets the goals that were stipulated in the RFP document. We look at their financial template, which is what we provided with the RFP. It includes the revenues, staffing expenses, food costs, and direct and indirect operating costs. And we also look at fees, commissions, and other elements of the financial package.

The financial bid receives a score point-wise, and for comparison's sake, we also create a separate financial spreadsheet model that has the retail revenues broken down by venue and bidder. We have a staffing tab that does the same thing by venue and bidder. It also breaks down the total cost by venue and management versus hourly staff.

We pull all of this information into a snapshot worksheet so that it's easy for administrators to take a quick look and compare. We have it organized by bidder, along with key categories highlighted, such as the board rate at a college or university and what that's going to cost them per student, per day. The type of meal plan offered comes into play here, as well.

We look at the projected commissions and take the percentage and the actual dollar amount that are in the bid sheet. We do this because one operator may have a higher percentage, but a lower projected return, and we want to be able to isolate those differences when we put it all in the snapshot.

We wrap up all of this information and come up with a total estimated remuneration, which includes all of those in-kind contributions, capital investments, and commissions. This enables the client to see the big-picture perspective of what that particular program, by that particular bidder, is going to cost and what kind of remuneration they can expect at the end of the year.

Nothing about this process is hidden from view. We clearly state what the bidder will be evaluated on, and memorialize all of the scoring criteria in the RFP so that the bidder is in the position to provide us with all of the necessary information.

The baseline for the weighted scoring system is typically three points per criteria. Points are awarded according to the information provided, but bidders can go past that by providing more information than what we've asked for. Alternatively, they will get a lower score if they don't comply with our guidelines.

Those points are tied into the actual weighted percentage table that is included in the RFP.

It's a true weighted score. For instance, one particular category could have a hundred possible points, but that may only relate to ten percent within the overall score because some other categories, such as financial bids, are worth more than categories such as labor and training practices.

Again, everything is explained in the RFP. We show how we will break down the bid submittal, look at each criteria, compare it, score it, and then feed that into a formulaic weighted table to give us a true, weighted score. In the end, we have created an equal comparison among the bidders.

Admittedly, this is a very time-consuming process on our end, but the result is a high quality product that comprehensively reviews all of the bids for our client.

Scoring systems such as ours are common in the industry, but what makes us unique is that not only do we develop a weighting system for each individual school we work with, but we also define the program with extreme specificity and memorialize both in the RFP.

Every base is covered, and there are no gaps to be found. Our method ensures the integrity of the bidding process and provides an incentive for the bidders to respond properly to the specific details in the program. We want to avoid ambiguity and make it perfectly clear what we expect and how important each criteria is.

Adversely, there have been times when bidders leave out information that we have requested, and without our review system, it would be extremely difficult to notice.

In one case, after breaking down a bidder's response, we found that they stated they would keep a particular location open until midnight, as the school requested, but when we compared it to their staffing matrix, we saw that they only staffed the location until eight p.m.

Now let's say that we didn't notice this discrepancy and signed a contract with them. Once they moved on campus and the school realized the error, then you know what the operator would say?

"Oops. We made a mistake. But instead of doing what we said we'd do for you, we can't now—that is, unless we charge you more or pay you less."

The deal is done, and the client has no leverage at all. They're at the mercy of the operator.

Our system is in place to ensure this never happens.

Our process will save you millions of dollars, and the scoring methodology is an important part of that process. As I mentioned before, you could probably find someone who can put together a dining program for you and write it all in an RFP. You could also probably find somebody to help you review the bid submissions. But you won't find anyone who will do it all for you with an equal level of passion, negotiating skill, and specificity—anyone, that is, other than David Porter and his dream team.

CHAPTER NINE

David's Top 10 Keys to Selling More Meal Plans

IS YOUR MEAL PLAN program the financial backbone of your campus dining services department?

The quick and simple answer is that if it's not, it should be.

There are so many misconceptions when it comes to meal plans and campus dining. Among the list is the belief that parents and students don't want to spend money on them, students think meal plans are over-priced, and the answer to low meal plan participation is to lower the price of the meal plan.

None of these statements is either true or helpful, and will only further the crisis of signing up, and keeping, students on your campus meal plan.

I'm here to address these misconceptions and illuminate what having the right meal plan can do for your school. But even more than that, I'm going to tell you how to achieve the optimum meal plan.

First, let's breeze through the basics.

Meal plans can vary widely from campus to campus, but most are some combination of declining balance—where students pay a certain amount of money for the semester and can use it at retail à la carte locations for meals, snacks, etc.—and/or a quantified number of meals per week, usually in increments of twenty-one, fourteen, or ten or a larger block of meals per semester, i.e., three hundred, two hundred, or one hundred fifty. Another, less common alternative is unlimited access dining, which we'll touch on later in the chapter.

After students enroll in their university of choice and it's finally time to sign up for housing, they're usually required to concurrently sign up for a meal plan.

An important thing to remember is that at this point, the parents are the customers. Not only are most students oblivious to meal plan particulars as incoming freshman, but it's the parents and/or Financial Aid who are footing the bill.

And how do parents pick which meal plan is best for Johnny or Susie?

In many cases, this is the first time their child is out of the house, and they don't want them to starve. Nor do they want to worry about them feeding themselves, so parents tend to purchase the largest plan available that presents itself as having the most options.

So then Johnny moves on campus and puts his parents' dollars to use. But what happens if the dining facilities are only open until seven and he doesn't eat dinner until nine? Students are on a different schedule, not like the nine-to-five format of the elders.

What if he realizes that he doesn't eat twenty-one meals each week? (In fact, statistics show that students eat around thirteen meals per week, on average). Or what if he finds himself at the end of a semester with either not enough declining balance food dollars left to spend, or hundreds of dollars left on his declining balance account that will disappear if he doesn't "burn through them" on convenience store offerings such as cases of water, Gatorade, and granola bars, the price of which is two or three times higher than what you would find in a supermarket or even a regular gas station?

In either case, Johnny will feel like the dining program has little or no value and that it is not working for him. There will be any number of reasons for this, least of which is the actual price of the meal plan; however, ninety-five percent of the time, Johnny and Susie's collective angst and negativity regarding the meal plan will manifest itself in some form of the following statement: "The meal plan is too expensive and I want to get off." Suddenly, Johnny is very interested in how much his dining program costs, but only because he's a dissatisfied customer who wants off because "it's not working for him."

That's when he'll call up Mom and Dad and say,

"Get me off the plan as soon as possible. It's not worth the money."

And so goes the vicious cycle that hundreds of universities across the country find themselves in, without ever really understanding why. It's the "buy high, buy down, and get off" model that will drive your dining program into the ground.

Parents buy the largest meal plan for their students, and halfway through the year, Johnny will tell them to buy less because he's not using all of it up. And then finally, because your customers feel like they are getting such a bad deal, they will opt out of the meal plan program completely. You know the drill.

Another factor that schools think influence meal plan enrollment are apartment dwellers who have kitchens. It is assumed that just because people have kitchens, they're going to use them. But the truth is, kitchens are like hotel swimming pools. Most travelers will opt for a hotel that has a swimming pool even though most that do so will never use the pool. I believe the same applies to students living in apartments with kitchens. Most students who have an apartment with a kitchen simply don't have the time or the desire to plan their own meals, shop for food, cook, and clean up every day.

In either case, what a successful voluntary, full

semester meal plan high participation boils down to is value. A meal plan is nothing more and nothing less than a "method of payment." If students feel like they're getting value from their dining program, then not only will they want to stay on it when it's no longer mandatory, but they'll continue to enroll year after year—apartment kitchen, or not.

Often times, schools think that when students complain about the price of their meal plan, the solution is to lower the price. Over the past twenty-two years as a consultant, I have witnessed hundreds of administrators wrapping themselves around a pole trying to come up with new meal plans, usually at a lower price. In my opinion, they're only trying to make a less than desirable dining program more desirable by charging less for it. The fact is, it doesn't matter how much a meal plan costs—if the dining program does not work for the student and, in turn, the student does not feel that it is a good value, then it will always be considered a rip-off.

So how do you create value? How do you strengthen the financial backbone of your dining services revenue?

It depends on a balance of a variety of factors, which I've narrowed down to ten target areas. So without further ado, I present to you "David's Top Ten Tips for Optimizing Meal Plan Participation on Your Campus."

TIP 1
Fix your dining program.

Is the problem the meal plan structure, or is the problem in the value of your program? Nine times out of ten, I can tell you that the problem is the program. If you're not offering what they're looking for in menu variety and selection, method(s) of service, location, ambience, hours of operation, operating days per year, and social engagement opportunities, then they'll find other ways to meet these needs off campus. I can assure you that when students are beating a drum to be able to spend meal plan money off campus in local establishments, it has little or nothing to do with the "meal plan." It has everything to do with the school's failure to meet those basic needs on campus. They don't want to spend money on something they view as inferior, just as you don't want to offer an inferior program.

Some universities will actually accommodate students' off-campus preferences by allowing them to spend their dining dollars at these locations. This is like a dirty little secret or cancer to your dining program. The students seem happy because they can finally get what they want, when they want it (using their meal plan). Some administrators who supported the idea are happy because students are happy; however, over time you will watch the underpinnings of the financial foundation of your dining program erode away because of the caustic effect this has on your financial statements and dining performance as an auxiliary service.

Remember when Ross Perot waxed poetic about the "sucking sound" we would all hear going from the USA across the Mexican boarder? This may be an effective strategy if your goal is to get out of the dining services business during certain day parts; otherwise, you might want to invest in a set of earplugs.

TIP 2
Find out what your customers want.

Steve Jobs once said that he never asked customers what they wanted. He would just decide. What he did do, however, was qualitative research, and that's what I recommend for developing your best dining program, and in turn, optimizing your meal plan participation. Conduct research. Do face-to-face interviews and focus groups. Sit down with the Director of Student Life, students, and administrators. Talk to the Director of Admissions. This may be your best snapshot of how successful, or unsuccessful, your dining program really is. Ask them if they steer the students to, or away from, the dining facilities. Ask Housing if the dining program influences a student's decision to move off campus, find out from Student Life if the social heartbeat of your campus revolves around the occasional "flash mob." Their answers tell all.

What people do, in my opinion, is the best indicator of what they will do. This is important to remember when conducting the interviews, and is also why I never ask the students what they want. If I were to ask them what they want, they'll probably say things that may sound politically correct and extremely attractive, but would never actually be used.

Ask students and faculty what their habits are. Where do they go for lunch? What time do they take their meals? Their answers will help you figure out what's missing on campus, and how you could create a program that is valuable to its customers.

TIP 3
Make your program work for your customers.

There's not a person who goes to Whole Foods or goes into an Apple store to save money. And yet Whole Foods and Apple are wildly successful. Why? Because people believe they're getting a compelling value when they go there. Where are the drumbeats and pleas from students to save money now?

How do you determine the value price equation for your dining services that will essentially make concerns for your meal plan price moot? By adjusting the hours to fit the students' lifestyles. By making methods of payment easy—accepting credit cards and cash. By giving them beautiful facilities where they can enjoy their food and create, and nurture, relationships with friends. These things work for the customer and encourage them to come back for more.

I like to equate it to creating a gravitational social pull toward dining every day. Starbucks has done it, Apple has done it, even Walmart has done it. We need to create the "it" factor for your dining experience. Food and meal plan pricing are essentially part of the supporting cast that reinforces this experience and this "it" factor on a daily basis throughout the academic year.

TIP 4
Enhance or create appropriate meal plans.

Let's assume that the program is perfect, and students are excited to participate. Now it's time to formulate a method of payment (meal plan) in order to create the revenue base necessary and to give students the ability to reap the benefits of your world-class dining program. Do you want declining balance? Unlimited access? Weekly or per semester block meals? Should options be mandatory and vary between classes? What combination is right for your campus? Again, you will find the answer to these questions through the qualitative data you gather from students, faculty, and staff.

TIP 5
Consider the value proposition.

Value is emotion. We all have it and we all experience it. This has everything to do with your gut—and your customer's gut—when you ask yourself, "Is this a good deal?" And, truth be told, the pit of your stomach answers this question before the cortex of your brain even asks.

If you paid $1500 for a Toshiba laptop, you'd probably feel ripped off about your purchase. But if you paid $1500 for a MacBook Pro that performed similar functions that you needed, you'd probably feel good about your purchase.

Does this have anything to do with your budget? No, obviously not. Does it have anything to do with MacBook owning a technological edge over Toshiba? That's also a no—both devices basically do the exact same thing. The difference is that MacBook is perceived as having value and that extra "oomph" that enables you to fork over hundreds more for basically the same product.

When it comes to meal plans, I have narrowed down the value proposition to two fundamental categories. One is consumption-driven, or how much you can get with the amount you have to get it with. If a student has twenty-one meals per week and on average has about six unused meals at the end of each week, how will he "feel" about the inherent value of this meal plan? If they have too much left over, will they feel ripped off?

The other category is access-driven. The value there is not about how much you get with what you have to get it with, but it's about the ability to go and eat whenever you want and eat as much or as little as you want based on your lifestyle. The inherent value is "I can if I want to, even if I don't want to."

This is where another myth muddies the water: Unlimited dining means that students will stuff themselves with food. This simply isn't true. As I discussed earlier in the book, students actually eat smarter, and in many cases eat less, when they know the kitchen is always open, and they don't have to make the most out of the two meals they would have been allotted under a consumption-driven program. That means not only healthier students, but lower food costs for the school and far less waste. It's a strange phenomenon. When students purchase traditional meal plans with fewer meals per week, it creates an incentive to eat more food with each swipe, hungry or not, in order to get the "biggest bang for their swipe."

TIP 6
Combine and enhance the meal program.

Entice customers to want to voluntarily stay on and buy up. I would like to pose a challenge to you right now. Take a minute, get a pencil and paper, and write down all of the establishments you have visited over the past ten years that have encouraged you to "buy down." Include movie theater concessions, newsstands at the airport, fast food, casual and fine dining restaurants, resorts, retail outlets, etc. Make the list as long as you wish, but I'm guessing you'll only have one place on the list—your campus meal plan.

When we reinvent your dining program and optimize the social architecture that in turn creates a compelling value and a colossal distinction for your school, we can also create a paradigm shift for meal plans. The brass ring is when we create meal plans that are more expensive and that customers voluntarily buy up to, because they are "worth it." And with my list of tips in mind, it's completely possible.

TIP 7
Make payment options user-friendly.

Make it easy for customers to sign up and add money to their meal plans, even with financial aid. Not long ago, I visited a school that sold most of their food offerings on carts positioned throughout campus. I went to grab a coffee from one of these carts, but was turned away because I didn't have cash. They seemed proud of the fact that they had ATM machines two buildings away where I could withdraw money, then come back and purchase a cup of coffee. That was a huge inconvenience and in this electronic day and age, I imagine it was a big problem for sales. They lost my sale.

The hardest part of purchasing should be choosing between the Italian sub sandwich or tuna salad—never remembering to bring the correct form of payment.

TIP 8
Keep your menu and facilities aesthetically pleasing and enticing.

Renovate tired dining facilities. Make the space multi-purpose for student and dining events. Gone are the days of hangar-like cafeterias. We've seen, and implemented, dining facilities with a variety of seating options, including lounge areas, high-top tables, banquettes, and more. Very retail and restaurant-like. Create a facility where students want to come to see and be seen, or as one of my professional colleagues said recently, C.H.O. Row.

TIP 9
Continually do your homework.

Seek input from meal plan and non-meal plan holders. Hire a consultant to conduct annual campus-wide surveys. Do your financial diligence. Look at your performance, staffing matrices, and financial impact of what you're programmatically looking to change. Never be afraid to adjust to meet the needs of your students. Adaptability is integral to continued success.

TIP 10
Make your meal plans and dining program a competitive advantage for your school.

Ultimately, this will help with recruitment, retention, and alumni relations—the three Rs. When a prospective student sees a bustling dining venue that brings students together, helps them make friends, and helps with alumni relations, then that will enhance the overall value.

In the end, we don't want students to move off campus because the meal plan sucks. In the end, we want them to say, "This is a great amenity for living on campus! What a great meal plan, and what a great value!" This will result in students voluntarily purchasing full meal plans after they move into off-campus apartments with full kitchens.

Follow these ten tips and you're headed in the right direction. In the next chapter, I'll discuss how you can really knock it out of the park with design.

CHAPTER TEN

Designing Your Destination

THE DESIGN OF YOUR dining facilities is the ultimate manifestation of your optimum program. It's the icing on the cake, the shining star on the top of the hill. But the importance of design goes beyond what's pleasing to the eye. In order for the design to be successful, it must above all functionally support the program that has been determined to best serve the students.

When we are hired to design a facility, the first thing we do is determine what the demand is going to be. How many people will we have to serve and within what period of time? This calculation includes residents, non-residents, commuter students, visitors, faculty, and staff.

This is not just an important estimate for the immediate future, but it is also very telling for what is to come.

Most dining facilities have a life span of anywhere between fifteen to thirty years. And let's face it, if you're going to invest millions of dollars in a new dining hall, then it had better last thirty years, right?

It's important to understand what the demand is going to be like over those next thirty years so that you can spend those decades rejoicing in your good investment instead of wringing your hands with regret.

Figures such as projected student enrollment growth, new housing plans, and new building projects help to paint a picture of what the future will look like. Are they going to add more beds on campus? Remove some? Depending on the answer, you may need to build up, or build down.

The next step is to factor in the new dining program. What will the concept, methods of service, menu, and hours of operation be like? Will breakfast be from seven to nine, lunch from eleven to two, and dinner from five to eight? If so, that means that the facilities will have to be programmed and designed for peak demand, and that could translate into a bigger serving area with a larger dining room that can hold more students. If more students are going to come in a short period of time, then you'll need to have enough space for them to all sit down.

Or maybe your dining program calls for round-the-clock hours of operation. That gives the students the flexibility to not have to come within a limited period of time. You'll still experience peak demand and busy periods, but they're not as busy and the demand is spread out over longer periods of time. So that may translate into the need for a smaller dining room.

It is important to be as specific as possible when it comes to the kind of space you need because renovations cost money. The cost of redoing a facility is based on square footage. Let's say a facility needs another one thousand square feet added to the dining room. At $300 per square foot, you want to make sure you have the estimate correct the first time around!

Dining facility design has changed dramatically over the past thirty years. Back in the day, venues were typically divided in half. Half would be devoted to the dining room, and the other half would go to the kitchen and serving area.

Of that half devoted to the kitchen and serving area, two-thirds of that space was dedicated to the kitchen, hidden behind masonry block walls. That means that only one-third of that space was in view of students— hence the term "mystery meat," because who really knew where it came from anyway?

Today, all of that has changed. Gone are the days of mystery meat and gone are the days of cooking behind the curtain.

Instead of two-thirds of the venue space going to

the kitchen, that square footage has now shifted to support the serving area where the final steps of production take place in direct view of the customer.

Our dining culture has shifted toward one of display cooking or "eatertainment." People love to know where their food comes from, how it's prepared, and the person who prepares it. Not only is this entertaining to those who watch, but it also communicates that the food is freshly produced.

Kitchen staff also respond very positively to presentation dining. Statistics show that there is less staff turnover in such facilities. Instead of being hidden in the kitchen, they're now a part of the cast. It boosts job morale and makes people excited to be a part of the team. It's almost like a mini theatre in the round as they chop, grill, stir-fry, and sear in front of crowds of onlookers shuffling by to select their food.

Hours of operation and the level of demand are also very important to consider should you choose to emphasize display cooking. As I mentioned, if your dining hall is open 24/7, then there will be some very slow times. The challenge then becomes how to design a facility so that when it is slow, you can go to a cook-to-order mode. Furthermore, how the stations are positioned adjacent to one another could have a chilling effect on labor. We can design these stations so that during slow periods, they can stay open but labor can move between them. Some designs require dedicated staff regardless of the level of business in order to stay open.

The answer is to design that station so that not only can you produce ahead in anticipation of high volume busy times, but you can also reduce to cook-to-order during slow times. In this case, it helps to co-locate these platforms to that it's easy for staff to move from one to the other. This helps to modulate your staff in busy and slow times alike without closing down stations while you are open for business.

Another challenge is this notion of anytime dining versus à la carte. Á la carte dining involves any combination of pre-packaged or made-to-order food where each station has its own register. So the customer selects their food, then pays and sits down.

With anytime dining, once the meal plan has been purchased, the student does not ever pay again throughout the semester. They enter the dining room with a swipe of their card, like a health club membership. They can come and go from the dining room and dining stations as many times as they want. They can grab a glass of milk, and then go back for a banana later if they want a snack. It's a great solution that students find really satisfying because of its convenience and value proposition.

However, I've found that a lot of schools want to

promote à la carte dining under the belief that it's a trend that students want. Or maybe they're sold on anytime dining, but they're worried about committing to that direction and without a major renovation have the option of switching to à la carte dining.

I advise clients who find themselves at this crossroads to follow through with the anytime dining facility, because we can simply design the dining venue in such a way that would allow for an easy transition to à la carte dining, if they so choose to go that route at any time in the future.

It's also important to understand if the facility will be used for non-food related purposes. Does it need to be multipurpose? Will it be used for catering? Student programming? Do they need a venue for summer camps? Corporate activities?

These are just a few of the issues that are taken into consideration when looking at the program, demand, and cost. But there are even more issues that often mislead decision makers into spending money and getting the least results.

An outdated facility is one of the biggest issues—and greatest embarrassments for a school.

There's nothing worse than parents leaving the school with a negative impression just because your dining hall is behind a few decades. So people often go for a quick fix. But that quick fix ends up being more expensive and creates a greater problem than it would have if the university had taken the time to reevaluate their program in the first place.

Determine what should the program be. What is the business model going to be? What is the method of service? What are the expectations in terms of who you want to participate and when you want them to participate?

Once those criteria are established, then we can develop a design for you to make sure your plan will be functionally supported.

Oftentimes, the price tag on much-needed renovations will send officials running for the hills. That's when it's crucial to have the empirical data that our planning efforts can provide.

Let's say you need $20 million to renovate your facilities. That's enough to make anyone's jaw drop. But if you could prove that those renovations would lead to an additional $30 million in debt service, then the initial investment is undeniably worth it.

If you can provide the empirical data—the revenue and expense projections, the labor costs, etc.—then your chances of getting the support you need to redesign your facilities are that much stronger.

Again, I encourage anyone who is going through this process to be wary of using your food operator as a planning or design consultant. Companies such as Aramark will act as your consultant, and just as they'll tell you what your program should be, they will also provide a list of contractors and architects who will do a great job for your school.

Maybe they will do a great job, but these people will source procurement of services and equipment through their purchasing channels. That means that instead of being competitively bid, all of your purchases may be forced through one vendor.

Let's say you have $2 million worth of food service equipment. You have the option of either competitively bidding it among several kitchen equipment contractors, or going through one of the big corporation's procurement channels. Which option do you think will get you the better financial package?

By competitively bidding the equipment, you'll get the same product, but save yourself ten to twenty percent on the overall price. And twenty percent of that $2 million is no small potatoes.

Another thing we will provide you with is a blueprint for your school's social architecture. And that is something that the operator or architect cannot do. That is because the social architecture I refer to is a product of how the entire dining program is conceived and developed. In most cases when an architect gets on board, that part of the process, good, bad, or ugly, has been completed.

Part of social architecture is what I call "visual listening." When you go into a space, the architecture communicates something to you emotionally about the location or institution. Those emotions have the power to connect the student to your institution and keep the student coming back not just over the four years that they're there, but for the rest of their lives as loyal alumni.

As an institute of higher learning with your own distinct philosophy and mission statement, your dining hall represents more than just food service. What do you want to communicate? What do you want to achieve? How do you want your students to feel about you?

CHAPTER ELEVEN

The High Cost of Low Education

ACCORDING TO *USA TODAY*, kids who have a college degree enter the market with an average salary starting at $56K per year. Kids who have nothing more than a high school degree get into the market with an average salary of $21K per year. See how expensive it is to *not* go to college?

Project that out over forty-four years (assuming a retirement age of sixty-five), with an annual inflation rate of 2.5 percent, and by not advancing to college, you have just turned your back on over $2,700,000.00 in income. Now, the $30K you might have to take out in student loans seems like peanuts in comparison. With numbers like that, why would ANYONE think twice about attending college?

If I could once again channel one of my favorite comedy duos, Seth and Amy from *SNL*—"Really??? No...Really!!!"

Is there anyone on the planet who would not take that return on investment? Since you are betting on yourself, the odds of success are stacked in your favor. A compromise for those who need one might sound like this: Live like a high school grad, earn like a college grad. That sounds like a middle-class American Dream to me!

A president of a small college in the Midwest recently shared with me that today, a young person can get a degree online in the basement of their parents' house. However, he speculated, will that person be equipped to succeed in the corporate environment? You probably do not have to think long to come up with his answer.

Arguably, the thing that is exclusive to brick-and-mortar colleges is the "classroom outside of the classroom." This classroom is as compelling as the academic classroom, and it can offer something more: real face-to-face interactions with real people. That's something you just can't get on Facebook or Instagram.

The classroom outside the classroom is a social interaction incubator that facilitates and nurtures individual students to learn about time management, problem solving, and how to interact with other people. It's about learning how to socially navigate situations, maybe ones that even make you uncomfortable.

It's a smart and important initiative, and I'll tell

you a story to illustrate why: On a recent episode of *60 Minutes*, a young, fifteen-year-old boy was featured for developing an early screening test for pancreatic cancer. Clearly, this young man had an IQ off the wall and knew how to use it. But what I found fascinating was when the interviewer asked the boy if he realized how much of a genius he was.

The young man responded that if all he had were intelligence, the smartphone could easily replace him. What made him successful, he said, was that he knew how to be creative. He knew how to work with people, collaborate, and figure out solutions.

In the blockbuster television show, *Breaking Bad,* the lead character is a genius Nobel Prize-winning chemistry teacher, who later in life finds himself unable to earn enough money to pay his bills and support his family, and so he turns to making drugs. Clearly in this case, IQ and pure academic achievement is no guarantee for "the good life." In fact, if he had been able to negotiate with former business partners, he would have been a very wealthy man, indeed. However, he burned bridges, cut ties, and was consequently left to struggle on his own.

If only Walter White had known what this fifteen-year-old boy has already figured out: the collection of facts and knowledge accumulated through study isn't your real worth; rather, it is your experience working with people face-to-face. This teenager knows what most of us don't realize until long after graduation!

Every career counselor I have ever encountered has said that networking and building meaningful personal and professional relationships is essential to building professional success.

York University in Toronto is changing the game with their experiment called "flipping the classroom." Instead of gathering in a lecture hall or classroom to listen to a lecture, students watch lectures at home (on or off campus) on their laptop. The actual classroom component is comprised of group project study work. York knows how valuable it is for these students not just to be book smart, but to know how to socially collaborate, problem-solve, and work together, too.

The classroom outside the classroom is as important—and I believe that for the majority of college graduates is *more* important—to their post-graduation professional success than the academic classroom. What I'm here to suggest, however, is that the most important daily driver of socially potent face-to-face interactions, and all of the benefits that come from those social interactions for students and the colleges as well, has to do with—yes, you guessed it—the social architecture of dining and learning.

If college is the students' home away from home, then, like the home they grew up in, where food is served (dining) is also the epicenter of their social life at school—if, that is, it is programmed and developed properly.

In Bill Bishop's book *The Big Sort*, he describes how in our society we tend to sort ourselves into like-minded groups and belief systems right down to the cities, towns, and neighborhoods where we choose to live throughout our lives. He also describes the debilitating consequences of this that can take the form of social groups of various beliefs that adamantly refuse to consider that there are other Americans who may have differing personal, professional, religious or family belief systems, and lack the ability or willingness to empathize and compromise. Plenty of examples of this paralyzing form of polarization are evident in our Congress today.

The 24/7 socially rich college dining learning experience is perhaps the last "Big Mix" socially, where students make friends with the broadest and most diverse group of people. It's a fun, safe and wholesome environment where they can get to know people with different belief systems, lifestyles, and backgrounds, and engage in responsible and safe behavior. And it's fun because they're not under the watchful eye of a parent who scolds them if they say something politically incorrect or radical. It's a place where people can feel included and free to express themselves.

The college social experience may not change the student's belief system, but if they've got a friend who subscribes to a different paradigm, then maybe that will instill in them an open-mindedness that they will carry through life. And that makes for a better future for us all.

But the defining factor of what I'm about to suggest is different from the previous chapters of this book in that I'm not talking about just a dining hall. I'm suggesting that we combine the experience of the classroom outside the classroom and the social atmosphere of the dining hall, which has resulted in what I have created and developed as the next generation of dining on college campuses, "the dining-learning commons." What I have developed for colleges and universities will revolutionize how student centers and dining is programmed and developed on campuses throughout North America.

You want students to come to your campus, and you want them to stay on your campus. You want to distinguish yourself from the plethora of other colleges that offer higher education. And you want them to stay and spend on your campus. If you want students to take on debt in order to commit to your physical campus, then you've got to give them something they can't get anywhere else.

The dining-learning commons is the lynchpin of my groundbreaking new strategy.

The dining-learning commons gives students the opportunity to connect, and gives you the ability to meet the needs of your students. It's not so much about the food, although the food is central. It's the social connectivity. That's the real Holy Grail. That's the power. And that's what can be achieved in the dining-learning commons. And that's exactly what I'm going to detail in the following chapter.

CHAPTER TWELVE

Facebook Sucks—Now Let's Get a Life

IN THE FIFTEEN SECONDS it takes to shake someone's hand and look into their eyes, I will learn more about who they are as a person than I would spending hours scrolling and clicking through their Facebook page. In America, we want instant gratification when it comes to satisfying our hunger for food that we like to consume throughout the day/evening—that's why we're called a "Fast Food nation," and apparently, if the numbers don't lie, we are a Facebook nation, too.

In the same way that Morgan Spurlock weighed in on the effects of fast food on the biochemical health of the human body in his documentary, I'm weighing in on the effects of a primary diet of Facebook on our ability to establish and develop healthy personal and professional relationships as individuals.

The population spends billions of dollars on fast food and trillions of minutes on Facebook. We all have a fundamental need to eat, even if we choose "junk food," and we all have a fundamental need to connect to one another, even if the only choice made easily available to us is "junk social."

By "junk social," I'm referring to those fast food establishments of social media called Facebook, Instagram, and Twitter—a place where you can update the cyber world on your every move and post selfie after selfie. But unless you're auditioning for the part of Daisy or Donald Duck in the next Disney movie, those pictures of you mastering the fine art of the "duck face" on Instagram have all been for naught. We all enjoy our guilty pleasures, the gossip rags in the supermarket line, and the occasional reality show (nobody would admit they watched Jerry Springer, but somehow his ratings were off the charts... hmmm). But just like the consumption of "empty calories," don't make the mistake that just because everybody does it, social media is the be-all and end-all of the development of meaningful relationships that will serve you the best throughout your life. Are there better ways to develop the social skills you will need to succeed?

Career counselors seem united in the opinion that in order to secure a good job, you have to build a professional network. They also say that about eighty to ninety percent of communication between people, especially prospective employers and those looking for a job, is nonverbal.

In other words, it's your body language—how you present yourself, your facial expressions, the look in your eyes, how you have groomed yourself, your hygiene, the questions you ask, your ability to listen, how you verbally answer questions, how you react to tough questions—that distinguish you from all the other prospective employees.

Do the tone and timber of your words reconcile with your nonverbal facial and body cues? Are you squirming, do you project an air of self-confidence, what does the way you greet the people you are meeting with mean, and what kind of impression does your handshake make? Do you come off as civil, do you have good manners, what about your etiquette? Is there a smile on your face, do you seem interested in what the other person is saying?

If you don't know the answer to a question, can you be honest, seem sincere, and admit it to another person in real time? Can you deal with face-to-face rejection gracefully? Are you likeable? Do you have the emotional intelligence to be able to read another person's nonverbal cues and listen to their verbal communication, and when you sense they are uncomfortable, then thoughtfully and with confidence respond to them in a manner that makes them more comfortable?

In spite of the explosion and exponential growth of people of all ages participating in all of the various forms of electronic social media, face-to-face social interaction is the answer if our goal is to have a diet of healthy social interactions that lead to success in our lives through meaningful personal and professional relationships.

Social isolation is debilitating to the human emotional, spiritual, and physical condition. I was in Hartford, Connecticut on the eve of the one-year anniversary of the Newtown tragedy. The local news featured families and how they have been coping. One family interviewed was very involved with an advocacy group that is working towards the reduction and elimination of social isolation.

Maslow ranks the fundamental human need to socially connect as number three on his hierarchy of needs. Mother Teresa said that our hunger for love and affirmation is greater than our hunger for food. Facebook does not get credit for creating the need to socially connect, just as McDonald's does not get the credit for creating the need for humans to eat. As a fundamental part of the human condition, however, Facebook does get credit for developing a software application combined with the Internet to meet that fundamental human craving to connect to another person(s).

Have you ever heard the saying that instant

gratification is not fast enough? If you don't believe me, next time you are in a public place, look left and right and see how often everyone around you is checking their handheld device to be the first to keep up on the second-to-second lives of 500 of their closest friends. My belief is that, given the opportunity to connect in a socially rich, face-to-face environment, students will choose to lean into their conversations with one another instead of immersing themselves in their smartphones. But it takes the right program, venue, and atmosphere to do so—and that's exactly why I created the next generation dining-learning commons.

So how does this translate into that $2,700,000.00 of income? Last year, the CFO at Texas Tech University in Lubbock stated that their research shows that students who live and dine on campus have higher GPAs and graduation rates than those who don't.

The advice I hear students passing on to new or prospective students is that the two most important things to do to be successful in college are number one: socially engage; and number two: develop a study plan that you stick to in order to get your homework done.

The dining-learning commons is a place where students can do both. It's a fusion of education, learning, socializing, and connecting. It meets a fundamental human need to feel connected and emotionally secure, versus the dreaded social isolation. Even those of us who consider ourselves "loners" may or may not reluctantly admit that it feels better when we are with a group of people that welcomes and accepts us for who we are. When we are connected, we grow and flourish; when we isolate, we shrivel and sometimes die... literally.

Next to their parents, handheld device, and maybe siblings, what is the most important thing to a young person? Their FRIENDS. So when a student becomes immersed in a safe, socially wholesome and rich environment that promotes responsible behavior—such as my next generation dining-learning commons—it is a target-rich environment for making friends. Colleges and universities are well aware that the sooner new students connect socially (about 45 days into their first year on campus) and make friends, then the likelihood of them returning as a sophomore greatly increases. This is known as a school's "retention rate." Schools spend hundreds of millions of dollars to increase that retention rate. Why not invest that money in a program and permanent structure that will do the same job, but better? In the next chapter, I'll discuss how the dining-learning commons can help distinguish your campus from the plethora of others in what I call "The Big Dance."

CHAPTER FOURTEEN

The Big Dance

THERE HAS BEEN AN epidemic failure by university planners and administrators across North America to understand what is really happening with higher education. Campus planners misjudge and mismanage the development of safe, wholesome on-campus community spaces, student life, and the development of student centers and dining programs.

This has resulted in a misjudgment of the selection of what college or university will best equip sons and daughters to be successful on a personal and professional level, and graduate with the knowledge and social skills to become financially independent. I'm not happy to raise this question, but is it possible that some parents and prospective students choose a school like they choose a car? Is it practical or is it a status symbol? They all will get you from point A to point B, but what will it cost for the ride, and what will you have to show for it when it's done?

Malcom Gladwell, author of *The Tipping Point* and his most recent book, *David and Goliath*, said in a recent *60 Minutes* interview with Anderson Cooper that he graduated from University of Toronto, which cost approximately $6K per year, versus Harvard University, which would have cost him $60K per year. He asked Anderson, "Do you really believe that my education would have been ten times better by graduating Harvard versus University of Toronto?"

So the truth is, most of us are not getting into Harvard, Stanford, or the other Ivy League schools. So you have to ask yourself, is it about the price tag, the perceived status of the school's brand, the academics? There are quite literally hundreds of colleges and universities in North America that, once you graduate (check that box), will academically put you even with the hundreds of thousands of students who graduated the same year you did as it relates to the value of your diploma in the job market.

What do you want a college education to do for your son or daughter? The following is an excerpt from Denise Clark Pope's book *Doing School*: "A recent study by the American Council on Education shows that the number one goal for 74 percent of college freshmen is to be "very well off financially.""

Of the thousands of good school choices you have, with price tags for tuition ranging from almost free to more than $60,000 per year, which one do you choose that will create the greatest likelihood that your son or daughter will be able to secure a good job and be well off financially?

Many believe it is essential to develop the skills necessary to socially collaborate, problem-solve, and build a network to secure a good job. On a day-to-day basis there is nothing as intense and rich that provides opportunities for students to socially interact, relax, collaborate, problem-solve, and learn like the 24/7 dining-learning commons.

The epicenter of the classroom outside of the classroom is the 24/7 dining-learning commons. This "Social Coliseum" is to a campus what Fenway Park is to Boston, Yankee Stadium is to New York, Wrigley Field is to Chicago, or, on a much more granular level, what your kitchen is to your home. This is the Big Dance.

Luther sang that "a house is not a home unless the two of us are home." I sing that housing is not a home unless there is a 24/7 social vortex (AKA "the kitchen"). Each venue I just mentioned, including your kitchen at home, represents a focal point, or the heart and soul, for each community it is located in. Not one of these physical venues creates the need to connect, but how potent would a sense of community, connection, security, and social mobility be without them?

The dining-learning commons fundamentally evolves what forever has been primarily a dining transaction into what becomes primarily a social transaction with food playing a supporting role. You come to see and be seen, connect, socialize, hang out, study, collaborate, problem-solve, make new friends, AND dine. This Social Coliseum is synonymous with the David Porter next generation dining-learning commons and student center/unions.

Gone are the days of the cafeteria, dining hall, marché, and student centers, as we have known them. For students to become financially independent and to have the highest likelihood that they will not be returning to a parent's basement (with diploma framed and on the wall of that basement) anytime soon after graduation, the campus must provide wholesome and safe social spaces for the healthy social growth and development of students and the new community they represent (AKA their graduating class).

In the press release below, The University of Mary describes what "The Big Dance" will look like on their campus.

For Immediate Release
Tuesday, Oct. 22, 2013

Nationally Renowned Social Architect Spearheads Nation's First Dining-Learning Commons at Mary

University of Mary Introduces 24/7 Dining in Preparation for New Student Campus Center

BISMARCK, ND—*When it's completed, the University of Mary will be the first college or university in the nation with a "dining-learning commons." A dining-learning commons will allow students to gather in a "living room" like space, which will be the new Student Campus Center to be completed by the fall of 2015, to eat, socialize and study together at any time of the day or night they choose—much like they would do in their favorite room at home or a 24/7 hang out.*

It's also the subject of an upcoming book by the nation's preeminent social dining guru David Porter. Porter, author of The Porter Principles and the go-to person on social architecture for college and university campuses, is the mastermind behind this concept that really gives the students all the comforts of home—while on campus.

"It's social dining and learning re-imagined," added Elizabeth Condic, vice president for financial affairs at the University of Mary. *"Our lifestyles have changed over the years. No longer are we eating at seven in the morning, noon and at six in the evening during a typical day. We gather to eat at different times of the day to enjoy each other's conversation—it's no different for the life of a student—in fact it is probably more hectic and even less structured for them. Students should have access to this type of social dining space too for eating, learning and fellowship whenever they wish in a 24-hour period. We're excited to be the first to introduce this dining-learning commons experience."*

"Nothing is as profound as what is happening at the University of Mary," commented Porter. *"Not only do they have a rare 24/7 dining experience for their students, but they are taking it to another level that no other institution has dared to do. This concept allows students to network and connect with others in a wholesome and healthy social space on campus whenever they wish. It's the next generation of learning outside the classroom."*

Porter added, excelling academically is obviously important for the college student. But equally important, he says, is encouraging them to learn the life skills that form the foundation for a rich professional and personal life ahead. "The other side of a well-rounded college career is learning time management skills, career planning, building bonds with their campus, and friendships and meaningful relationships that will last a lifetime. Studies show that students who are socially connected to their campus have better GPAs, are personally and academically responsible, and have a better chance of graduating. This leading-edge thinking and endeavor by the University of Mary creates this new generation of social space."

The University of Mary is already one of only three campuses across the United States—and the only one north of the Mason-Dixon line—to currently offer a 24-hour, seven days a week dining services on campus for students. This service, that began this fall semester, allows students to have a meal plan and eat whenever they wish.

When Dorothy's world in the classic movie The Wizard of Oz transformed from black and white to Technicolor, she lit up and said, *"Toto, I have a feeling we are not in Kansas anymore"..."we must be over the rainbow."* This, I believe, is an apt description of the transformation awaiting you as the direct result of our groundbreaking approach to social programming and architecture to the day-to-day, face-to-face social life for your students and to the social landscape of your entire campus.

If that alone doesn't open your eyes to the potential to what these dining-learning commons can unlock on your campus, allow me to further break it down.

Most campuses already have a student center, and most of these centers already offer a mix of food options, whether it's an à la carte dining room, a branded food court, gourmet coffee and some kind of market or convenience store. But what I'm here to tell you is that—in the same way transforming your dining hall can transform your campus—you too can properly program and transform your student center into a 24/7 socially rich living room for your students and your campus.

It's a huge missed opportunity.

Student centers are typically buildings that are very busy during the day. They're bustling with activities, with resident students, non-resident students and resimuter students coming and going throughout the middle of the day, Monday through Friday, along with student programming and a vast array of student group related activity. There are plenty of reasons for people to go there. Some go for meetings and some for study sessions, while others hang out there because it is conveniently situated in or near the academic core of campus, and is close to where they take their classes.

But I also bet you that in 90 percent of the student unions in North America, you can shoot a cannon through them after four in the afternoon and on weekends.

On the nights and weekends that these student centers are almost empty relative to the student population at-large, it's for one simple reason.... The students do not want to go there. It's the same case as these underutilized dining halls. Students want a reason to stay on campus. They don't want to have to schlep off campus to get a slice of pizza and spend more money or to hang out, make friends, and study. If they had viable, strategically programmed options on campus, then you can bet they would spend their time—and money—there.

How does this play in to the social and long-term success opportunities I discussed in the previous chapter?

The strategic combination of dining and learning is the lynchpin to bring the students together. Once they're together, however, that's when the puzzle pieces connect in terms of what they learn academically and the emotional intelligence they learn in this classroom outside of the academic classroom.

That's why I have developed and named it the

dining-learning commons. It's a place where the two classroom worlds come together and unlock the optimum potential of achieving post-graduate financial independence for your son and/or daughter. All under one roof, you have a center for academic and social groups, and you have the unifying experience of sharing a meal.

How do you, as a campus, make the most of such a space?

By getting with the program. With our development and advent of the new, 24/7 dining-learning commons, there is so much more opportunity for learning, problem solving, and developing collaborative interpersonal relationship skills. This is a wholesome and safe space that fosters group study, collaboration and networking.

When the 24/7 dining-learning commons is made part of the student center, the social whole is exponentially greater than the sum of its parts.

Separate, you have a 24/7 dining-learning commons and a student center, which are both important elements. But together, when they work in the same building and you employ the systems I discussed earlier in the book, it becomes, in many cases for the first time in the history of the school, a 24/7 activated student-"centered" center.

In the hundreds of focus groups I have facilitated

over the past 24 years resident students have made it clear to me that the best place on campus to "be social" is centered around dining, especially nights and weekends. And when their school does not deliver this on-campus venue and program, they seek it off campus, at home on weekends if close enough, and/or attempt to replicate in their apartments with kitchens, or they just "keep to themselves."

One of the most frequently asked questions I've received throughout my career is, "David, how do we activate the building (a student center) on nights and weekends?"

This is the answer: give it the same treatment as you would your anytime dining-learning commons. Make it a place that will draw students in. As a social architect I can develop a program that, once implemented, meets fundamental human needs, thus giving them a compelling reason to go there. In my first edition I refer to this as a gravitational pull towards the venue(s).

The proof is in the pudding. I've worked with numerous campuses now, transforming their dining programs and activating their student centers with my groundbreaking, out-of-the-box recommendations. And in almost every case, though administrators may have initially found my recommendations impossible or "crazy", in the end, when our recommendations are implemented properly, they rave about how their campus has been transformed: student participation is up, retention rates are up, more students want to live and stay on campus, recruitment capture rates are higher, etc., etc., etc.

Students love it because they get to meet and hang out with their friends in a face-to-face environment, on their schedule, as a college student, anytime, day or night and weekends.

This will change the way colleges and universities do business and, more importantly, how parents and their sons and/or daughters select a college.

As you know, with student engagement, the retention rates go up. Recruitment capture rate goes up, because when a student goes to campus, the fact that your campus offers 24/7 unlimited dining gives your school a cross-applicant colossal distinction. The parents love it too, because they know their son or daughter will be safe in a 24/7, wholesome, on-campus dining commons that will feed their stomachs and minds like nothing they have ever experienced. Plus, they will never have to go elsewhere for food, nor need a penny more to supplement the meal plan that they have chosen.

And of course, the dining-learning center will make for better alumni. Not only will the experience on campus sharpen their social skills and create a wider social net, which in turn helps them with post-graduate success, but the connections they made, which were bolstered by the on-campus dining opportunities, give them a greater sense of belonging to the school. It becomes a place they'll want to return, and give back, to, as many of their happiest memories were spent on campus.

As college recruitment grows ever more competitive, I only see the dining-learning commons becoming ever more important in distinguishing and defining your campus. But the college arms race aside, it's a natural course of change. After all, the components are already in place: you have the students who want to be social and also eat well in a venue that is inviting and convenient. On the other hand, you have the space on campus—not to mention willing participants—to make it happen.

So why wait? Take advantage of the potential of your campus and graduate students who are equipped to take advantage of social skills, connections, and problem-solving skills that will ensure their financial independence regardless of the path they find themselves on.

The stakes have never been greater for higher education. Not unlike chemistry, there is no room for being selective regarding the combination of elements and compounds in order to achieve the desired result.

And, like chemistry, when innocuous elements are not combined properly, the results can be dismal.

In my next book, *The Porter Index*, due out fall 2014, I will unlock this "MoneyBall" code and show you how you and your sons and daughters can go about the process of selecting a college or university that may or may not pass the "eye candy" test, but will significantly increase the odds of your sons and daughters to succeed in life by setting out on a path that will permit them to achieve financial independence as the prerequisite for a better life......stay tuned.

CHAPTER FIFTEEN

Call to Action

ARE YOU FRUSTRATED WITH a lack of student engagement on your campus? Are you struggling with unsatisfactory student retention and recruitment capture rates? Do you want to improve the engagement of your alumni?

I asked you these questions at the beginning of the book, and my guess is that your answer has led you through to this very page. But the difference between then and now is that you've learned how dining can either significantly contribute to the problem, or to the solution. Maybe for the first time you now realize that you have a choice and you have control over how you choose to go about solving the problem, versus kicking the can down the road or just accepting the unacceptable.

You now know that the single, most powerful and effective tool you have to maximize the social engagement opportunities for your students, faculty, and staff on a daily basis is your dining program, and more importantly, how you go about organizing that program. Your dining facilities can contribute to that "seal the deal" moment for prospective freshmen visiting your campus, just as it can affect whether they choose to stay over the coming years. But how can you begin to address these issues if your dining just isn't working?

It starts with a complete reassessment of what your campus has to offer that will produce a meaningful experience for students, faculty, visitors, and staff.

Perhaps the information I've offered you has illustrated how difficult it can be to carry out this task without prior experience. Maybe you've even been struggling for years to develop new meal plans, rework your facilities, and come up with new ways to improve your program to no avail.

Now is the time to give us a call.

My team has worked with many institutions over the years to rectify the negative affects of an ailing dining program. We've helped hundreds of administrators and food service directors revamp their department so that they may reap the benefits of an optimum dining program. And we can do the same for you, but it all begins with one phone call.

Call me, invite me to your campus, and I will personally come on my own nickel for a face-to-face meeting. All I ask is that you gather your team of decision makers and allow me one day on your campus to answer all of your questions and discuss the opportunities for your dining program.

At the same time, I'll determine if the project is a good fit for my company. I'll spend time getting to know your facilities, history, and opportunities for improvement to see if it's the right kind of project for my team.

Neither size nor geographic location is a factor when it comes to the work that we do, and I encourage any university who is in need of our services to call us up. My offer to fly out and meet with your team still stands.

The only time I discourage you from calling is if you are currently rebidding the contract and it's already been sent out to bidders. Unfortunately, in that case it's too late for my team to perform the amount of research and due diligence necessary to make sure your institution is getting the optimum program and a sound contract. It would be like asking a doctor for a second opinion on your prognosis after your first doctor has you on the operating table.

In an ideal world, you would contact us at the start of the academic year before your current contract runs out. But we could even get the job done in as little as three months, if necessary. However, I encourage clients to give themselves plenty of time so that they can feel confident moving forward throughout the process.

Now that you know a little bit about what I do, you also know if the time is right to take steps to make your campus dining program as successful as can be. If the time is now, call me up. And when I say call me up, I mean it—I am available to talk to you, just as I will personally appear on your campus to discuss the opportunities that exist on your campus.

Want to learn more?
Please give me or Cézanne Grawehr a call at
410-451-3617
or email me at
david.porter@porterkhouwconsulting.com

Dedicated to
VIRGINIA D. PORTER
August 4, 1929 – August 7, 2011

Thank you, Mother.

*A mother's love for her child
is like nothing else in the world.
It knows no law, no pity.
It dares all things
and crushes down remorselessly
all that stands in its path.*
—Agatha Christie

Thank you, Dad.